# Teacher's Choice

## Across the Curriculum with Twelve Award-Winning Books

## by
## Sandy Terrell and Frank White

## illustrated by Sabrina Burroughs (Graphic Masters)

Cover by Ted Warren

Copyright © 1992, Good Apple

ISBN No. 0-86653-691-4

Printing No. 987654321

**Good Apple**
**1204 Buchanan St., Box 299**
**Carthage, IL 62321-0299**

SIMON & SCHUSTER *A Paramount Communications Company*

# Dedication

To our parents

GA1425

# Table of Contents

GA1425

# Introduction

*Teacher's Choice* is a literature unit that allows students to read and explore quality literature in cooperative learning groups. Students will be exposed to twelve books that will foster enthusiasm for reading. The activities that the teams work on, present and display will encourage other students to read the books.

The reading and interest level of the twelve novels range from fourth to ninth grade. The lessons and activities are developed to enable students to successfully participate in small group activities.

Each cooperative learning group reads one of the twelve books. They work cooperatively on twelve activities that span the curriculum. Each team works independently using their chosen book guide and follows specific instructions for the book. The activities are sequenced so the teams can read the first few chapters and do an activity that pertains to those chapters, read the next chapters of the book and do another activity and so on until they have read the entire book and done all the activities.

The teams earn points for each activity and keep track of their points on a poster. The points are cashed in at the end of the unit for incentives the teacher sets.

*Teacher's Choice* is developed to encourage students to read quality books and expand their knowledge across the curriculum.

GA1425

# How to Use and Prepare for
## *Teacher's Choice*

**Length of Unit**

*Teacher's Choice* can be played during your reading time as the literature component in your classroom. The unit is designed to be played in a three to five-week period. Pace the unit so it is comfortable and successful for you and your students.

***Teacher's Choice* Bulletin Board**

Make a banner across the top of the bulletin board to announce *Teacher's Choice* is coming soon. Post the Book Overviews (pages 8-11) so students can get acquainted with the books. As books are picked and teams organized, add the appropriate posters and sheets to the bulletin board. The Book Overviews should be taken down after the teams are formed to make room for other items. As you read further you will understand what materials will go on the bulletin board.

The bulletin board will become a focal point for *Teacher's Choice*. There are book posters and a reward poster that should be put on the bulletin board and stay for the duration of *Teacher's Choice*.

Teams will need a place to display their projects, and the bulletin board can be used for this purpose. There will be a lot of change in this board as the teams move along with their projects. Previous projects come down and new projects go on the bulletin board.

**Books**

Twelve award-winning books have been selected for students to explore. These titles are consistently regarded as quality work by teachers and students at these grade levels. The array of interest and reading levels insure that students will find a new book within these titles they will enjoy.

Have the students decide which book they want to read. It is the goal of *Teacher's Choice* for students to choose a book that they have not read. When presenting the book selections to the students, emphasize this goal.

**The books are as follows:**

grades 4-6   *The Secret of the Indian*
                 by Lynne Reid Banks

grades 4-6   *The Lion, the Witch and the Wardrobe*
                 by C.S. Lewis

grades 4-7   *Mrs. Frisby and the Rats of NIMH*
                 by Robert C. O'Brien

grades 4-8   *The Secret Garden*
                 by Frances Hodgson Burnett

grades 5-6   *The Cay*
                 by Theodore Taylor

grades 5-7   *Where the Red Fern Grows*
                 by Wilson Rawls

grades 5-8   *From the Mixed-Up Files of Mrs. Basil E. Frankweiler*
                 by E.L. Konigsburg

grades 5-8   *A Wrinkle in Time*
                 by Madeleine L'Engle

grades 6-7   *Danny, the Champion of the World*
                 by Roald Dahl

grades 6-7   *The Westing Game*
                 by Ellen Raskin

grades 6-9   *Sing Down the Moon*
                 by Scott O'Dell

grades 7-9   *Johnny Tremain*
                 by Esther Forbes

Each student will need a copy of the book that will be studied. Once the students select their books, ask students to help supply the books from their personal libraries at home, school or the public library.

GA1425

## Teams

It is advised to have four to six students on a team. In an average-sized class, there will probably be six to eight teams which means six to eight books will be explored this time you play *Teacher's Choice*.

Group students into cooperative learning teams according to the books they have selected. Students who would like to explore the same book are grouped together in one team as long as the size of the team is manageable in cooperative learning terms. If the teams appear too big, have students choose a second book and form smaller teams.

After the teams are formed, they should make up a team name. Discuss your rules for cooperative learning teams and do some modeling of teamwork to assure everyone is aware of and can abide by the cooperative rules.

## Projects

There are twelve projects for each book. The projects are organized so the students read a chapter or two then do a project. This process repeats until the entire book has been read and twelve projects completed. The projects encompass many curriculum areas: reading, math, language, science, social studies, physical education, art, cooking, dramatics, writing, music and handwriting.

Reproduce enough project pages so members on each team have a copy. For example, the students/team that has chosen *The Cay* will receive the project pages for *The Cay*. Wait to see what books have been selected before duplicating these pages. The project pages begin on page 28.

Teams should read and do projects in order beginning with chapter one of the book they have selected. As they finish a project they are to hand in the project to you. You will give them credits for each project. There is a credit box on each project chart for you to record the credits.

All the teams will have at least three projects that have to be presented in front of the entire class. Check the Activity Chart in this guide on page 12 to see when the presentations will occur in each book. This will give you an overview of what teams will be working on and in what order the projects occur. Advise your teams to schedule their presentations with you as soon as they realize they are going to have to present, so you can organize time slots for presentations.

GA1425

Cooking projects may need to be done at home if your classroom or school is not equipped for student cooking. If you have concerns about cooking projects at school or at home, adapt the cooking projects as needed.

Answers for a few of the projects have exact solutions. These answers are found on the Teacher Answer Sheet, pages 14-15.

## Credits

Credits is the system with which to evaluate projects. The scale of 1-10 is used and is based on 10 being superior. As the students finish each project, you will award credits to the project. If a project exceeds expectations, you have the option of awarding bonus credits to that project. Post the credits on the team book posters that you have tacked on the bulletin board.

At the end of *Teacher's Choice*, teams cash in their credits for incentives that you have outlined on the reward poster.

## Book Poster

A book poster for each book accompanies this guide. After the selection of the books has been made, duplicate one chart per selected book and tack up the charts on the bulletin board. As the teams finish each project, they add color to the space on the chart that headlines the project. You fill in the credits earned on the charts so teams can keep track of their credits. These book posters start on page 16.

## Reward Poster

The reward poster is filled in by you with an array of incentives that you have selected for rewarding the teams when *Teacher's Choice* is completed. Choose the prizes from the suggested list that you feel your students would most enjoy. List one or two rewards in each section of the reward poster. Feel free to add to the list any prizes special to your class.

Teams will pick rewards that total their credits. As you fill in rewards on the credit sheet, be aware that more enticing rewards, such as a team movie or pizza party should be worth many credits so teams are motivated to achieve at a high expectation level and produce quality projects. The reward poster is on page 13.

GA1425

A list of incentives for the reward poster follows only as examples. You will have many ideas of your own.

| | |
|---|---|
| a pizza party | bookmarks |
| candy bars | pass to library |
| extra free time | a week free of homework |
| a hug by the teacher | bubble gum/bubble blowing contest |
| a hot dog cookout | videotape of a favorite movie |
| popcorn | watermelon feed (seed spitting contests optional) |
| favorite stickers | |
| ice cream | sitting anywhere in the classroom for a week |
| | a day of student-supplied music during class |

## Materials

Basic classroom and art supplies are needed along with a few special items that may be needed from time to time. The teams can be responsible for these items.

The following books and poems are referred to in the student project pages and should be available:

- *Sherlock Holmes* by Sir Conan Doyle (various titles), referred to in *The Westing Game*

- *Charlie and the Chocolate Factory* by Raold Dahl, referred to in *Danny, the Champion of the World*

- *Charlotte's Web* by E.B. White, referred to in *Mrs. Frisby and the Rats of NIMH*

- *Call It Courage* by Armstrong Perry, referred to in *From the Mixed-Up Files of Mrs. Basil E. Frankweiler*

- *The Indian in the Cupboard* by Lynne Reid Banks, referred to in *From the Mixed-Up Files of Mrs. Basil E. Frankweiler*

- *Rascal* by Sterling North, referred to in *Where the Red Fern Grows*

- "The Midnight Ride of Paul Revere" by Henry Wadsworth Longfellow referred to in *Johnny Tremain*

GA1425

**Other Necessary/Useful Materials:**
- almanac
- encyclopedia
- newspaper
- compass
- square dance record
- atlas

**Analysis Page**

There is an analysis page for each book to evaluate comprehension and to expose students to higher order thinking skills. The teacher and teams may orally discuss the questions or include the entire class in each discussion. The analysis page can also be given to each student in the group and used as an individual written evaluation of each student, or the group can answer the questions as a team effort. Choose the best plan for your students. The analysis pages begin on page 172.

GA1425

# Time Frame

The following sample time schedule will help organize *Teacher's Choice*. Adapt it to your needs and your students' needs.

**First Day**

1. Explain the overall idea of *Teacher's Choice*. Emphasize how *Teacher's Choice* will be a fun and exciting way to explore new books. Explain the book posters, projects, reward posters and other items pertinent to understanding *Teacher's Choice*.
2. You present the list of books available to explore from the Book Overviews. If you did not put them on the bulletin board at the beginning of the unit, feel free to read this information out loud to the students.
3. Students decide on the book they will explore. After book decisions have been made, find out from the students how many copies of the books they have and how many you will have to locate for class use.
4. Divide students into teams according to the books they are going to read. Space teams around the room so they will have adequate working space.
5. Have students talk about how they think they will get along on a team project. Lead a brief discussion to express ways they could successfully work together.
6. Have teams select a team name.
7. Teacher preparation for the next day of *Teacher's Choice*:
   Duplicate and staple copies of the book projects for each team.
   Duplicate the appropriate book posters and put them on the *Teacher's Choice* bulletin board. Put up reward poster if it is not already on the bulletin board.

**Following Days**

1. Students work in teams. Every student should have a copy of the book on which their team is working.
2. Hand out project guides. Give teams a time frame in which they will work on their reading projects.
3. Teams work on reading their books and starting projects. Allow some reading time to get started on the books and/or assign some of the reading as homework.
4. Teams work on their projects.
5. As teams complete projects, they color that space on their book poster, and you post their credits in the correct section of the book poster. Your main duties now are to keep the posters on the *Teacher's Choice* bulletin board updated. Teams will usually run fairly independently from this point.

# Book Overviews

**The Secret of the Indian by Lynne Reid Banks**

It all started when Omri discovered he could bring to life the miniature plastic Indian, the American cowboy, and other toy figures. But after a year Omri never would have guessed that it would start all over again! The responsibilities of food and shelter for his tiny friends and the enormous stress that grown-ups would discover the unbelievable scene in his room was too much for Omri. The fact that new people find out about the magic in Omri's room and the incredible transport of Patrick and Omri back to the old American West add suspense to the story.

People die while others teeter on the brink of death. When and how will it all stop without disrupting the past history of the world? The book is filled with realism as the reader is caught up in the turmoil that grows and grows in Omri's attic bedroom.

**The Lion, the Witch and the Wardrobe by C.S. Lewis**

The adventures of Narnia begin with an innocent peek into a wardrobe that changes the lives of four children forever. The perils of adventure engulf the children as they return to Narnia through the soft warm furs that turn into rough, cold tree branches. They are faced with overpowering the White Witch and saving a kingdom, but one of them is a traitor. Who could it be? Battles are waged and fought as creatures turn into stone for many years. Only one can return and save the kingdom. But is it too late? Can Narnia be saved? With willpower, determination and devotion, many fight against evil, but is it enough? Isn't right supposed to conquer in the end?

**Mrs. Frisby and the Rats of NIMH by Robert C. O'Brien**

Mrs. Frisby, an uncommon field mouse, is faced with a dilemma. Farmer Fitzgibbon would soon "plow under" Mrs. Frisby's winter home. With the illness of Timothy, her young son, moving day becomes a matter of life and death. Secrets of ill doing are uncovered as Mrs. Frisby desperately tries to save her child. Things that had happened to her dead husband are revealed to her and responsibilities that she thought she could never handle are passed on to her. Help from a very special group of rats, an encounter with Dragon (the fierce cat), and a very cunning plan are all woven together into this 1972 Newbery Medal story. The National Institute of Mental Health (NIMH) will never be the same.

GA1425

### The Secret Garden by Frances Hodgson Burnett

Mary is an unhappy orphan that is forced to live in the English home of a wealthy uncle, a man who has made no time for children since the untimely death of his wife who died during childbirth. There is a mysterious young boy found in the mansion who reigns over everyone but Mary. Secrets and other mysterious people run wild throughout this book. Mary finds a secret garden on the grounds that has been hidden in the minds of the old gardener and Mary's uncle for years. Life changes for all who become entangled with Mary's temperament and will to see things grow. Startling changes come over many of the characters in this book who are touched in some way by the secret garden.

### The Cay by Theodore Taylor

German submarines threaten the lives of the people on Curacao, a Dutch island off the coast of Venezuela in 1942. A young boy, Phillip, and his mother leave the island, but disaster hits the fleeing vessel. A shipwrecked Phillip shows his prejudices as he refuses help from Timothy, an old boat hand. As his life continues to depend on Timothy, Phillip learns that being blind can truly open one's mind. Phillip and Timothy struggle through natural and emotional disasters that make them both stronger in one sense and one of them weaker as death draws near. *The Cay* is a wonderful story of young and old, black and white and learning from each other. Some of the heartaches of survival are overcome while others are too enormous to comprehend.

### Where the Red Fern Grows by Wilson Rawls

This book is an unforgettable story of love and devotion between a boy and his dogs. Billy worked hard for the day when he could have his hounds. He and his dogs were rarely parted as they night hunted the old hills and river bottoms of the beautiful Ozarks. Billy, Old Dan and Little Ann were known across the hills and valleys as the hunting trio to beat. Some tried and failed, but in the end something else won out to the heartache of Billy. His family had commitments to keep, so life had to go on. This is an exciting tale of love and adventure that is magical in so many ways. The ending of this book is mixed with sadness and happiness that represents the end of some lives and the beginning of other lives.

GA1425

**From the Mixed-Up Files of Mrs. Basil E. Frankweiler by E.L. Konigsburg**
Claudia is unhappy with life at home and feels unappreciated. Desiring a change, Claudia enlists the help of Jamie, her penny-pinching younger brother, and together they have a "running away" adventure unlike any other. Living at the Metropolitan Museum of Art, they encounter an exhibit surrounded by mystery. Add to this mixture Mrs. Basil E. Frankweiler, a somewhat eccentric and very rich old lady who is at the center of the mystery, and you have a charming story about family relationships, changes and growing up that will delight the reader.

**A Wrinkle in Time by Madeleine L'Engle**
This book is a combination of science fiction, mystery, suspense and horror that starts off with the arrival of a most disturbing stranger. Meg Murry's father has been missing for some time, and people have formed many opinions and started dozens of rumors about his disappearance. But Meg never gives up hope that he will return. When the opportunity to go and find him arises, Meg and her intuitive brother "fly" at the chance to investigate. Little did they know just how far out they would travel. A new concept of a tesseract is explored by the human beings with not so human others as their guides. This Newbery Medal winner is hard to put down!

**Danny, the Champion of the World by Roald Dahl**
Danny is a young boy with a great treasure, a dad who is "Sparky." When Danny discovers his dad is a poacher (as is just about everyone in the district), he is shocked. This shock turns to enthusiasm when Danny discovers a way to help turn Mr. Victor Hazell's ill-famed pheasant shooting party into a farce. With the help of the doctor, the local constable, the Vicker's wife and, of course, his beloved dad, Danny proves himself as the "champion of the world."

### The Westing Game by Ellen Raskin

This exciting mystery pits the reader against the multimillionaire Samuel W. Westing. The characters and the clues are woven into a brilliant tapestry of mystery, adventure and intrigue. Sixteen players are possible heirs to Sam Westing's fortune. The sum of $200,000,000 is at stake in this "part mystery story, part play-along game and part do-it-yourself puzzle." Remember, nothing is what it seems to be. This 1978 Newbery Medal winner is delicious reading.

### Sing Down the Moon by Scott O'Dell

Bright Morning, a young Navajo girl, lives a relatively tranquil life in Canyon de Chelly. This tranquility is shattered by Spanish slavers, white soldiers, and a long, devastating march to Fort Sumner. Bright Morning's story is one of bravery as well as broken spirits, hope as well as broken promises, and the inner strength of one girl longing to return to her native way of life. The story shows us injustices through the sometimes stoic eyes of one whose human spirit cannot be broken.

### Johnny Tremain by Esther Forbes

Johnny Tremain, a young silversmith, gets caught up in the turbulent pre-Revolutionary War times of Boston. Following a terrible burn he receives on his hand, Johnny finds his lifelong occupation and desire suddenly stripped from him. After a period of adjustment he meets Rab, a confident young man involved with the young movement for American freedom. John and Samuel Adams, John Hancock, Paul Revere and James Otis all come to life as we view them through the eyes of Johnny Tremain. The Boston Tea Party and the Battle of Lexington become a living drama as we better understand the humanity and history of the events leading to America's Revolutionary War.

GA1425

# Activity Chart

The chart shows the exact order and presentation of activities for each book.

| | The Westing Game | A Wrinkle in Time | The Secret Garden | From the Mixed-Up Files of Mrs. Basil E. Frankweiler | Mrs. Frisby and the Rats of NIMH | The Secret of the Indian | Sing Down the Moon | The Cay | Where the Red Fern Grows | Danny, the Champion of World | Johnny Tremain | The Lion, the Witch and the Wardrobe |
|---|---|---|---|---|---|---|---|---|---|---|---|---|
| #1 | Art | Art | Lang. | Phy. Ed. | Cook* | Drama* | Cook* | Art | Drama* | Art* | Lang. | Art |
| #2 | Write | Drama* | Soc. St. | Math | Handwrit. | Math | Music* | Drama* | Soc. St. | Science | Music* | Soc. St.* |
| #3 | Handwrit. | Lang.* | Read* | Soc. St. | Read | Science | Science* | Soc. St. | Read | Lang. | Art* | Cook* |
| #4 | Cook | Science | Write* | Science* | Drama* | Phy. Ed.* | Soc. St.* | Write | Art* | Math | Write | Phy. Ed.* |
| #5 | Math | Cook* | Phy. Ed.* | Write | Lang.* | Write | Drama* | Cook* | Music* | Write | Phy. Ed.* | Handwrit. |
| #6 | Drama* | Phy. Ed.* | Art | Art | Music* | Read* | Handwrit. | Read | Write | Handwrit. | Soc. St.* | Music* |
| #7 | Science | Write* | Math | Handwrit. | Science* | Soc. St.* | Art | Science* | Handwrit.* | Music* | Science | Read* |
| #8 | Soc. St. | Math | Handwrit. | Lang. | Soc. St.* | Lang. | Phy. Ed.* | Math* | Math | Phy. Ed.* | Drama* | Math |
| #9 | Phy. Ed.* | Music* | Drama* | Drama* | Art | Cook | Read* | Lang.* | Cook* | Read | Handwrit. | Write |
| #10 | Music | Soc. St. | Cook | Read | Phy. Ed.* | Art | Write | Handwrit.* | Science | Soc. St. | Read* | Lang. |
| #11 | Read | Handwrit. | Science | Cook* | Write | Handwrit. | Lang. | Phy. Ed.* | Phy. Ed.* | Drama* | Math | Drama* |
| #12 | Lang. | Read | Music* | Music* | Math* | Music* | Math | Music* | Lang.* | Cook* | Cook* | Science |

*presentation or sharing

# Rewards

| | |
|---|---|
| | **120 Credits** |
| | **100 Credits** |
| | **80 Credits** |
| | **60 Credits** |
| | **40 Credits** |
| | **20 Credits** |

# Teacher Answer Sheet

Here are the answers to the projects that have exact answers.

**The Secret of the Indian**
Project 2 Math:

| | Pounds | Dollars | German Marks | Japenese Yen | What could you purchase with this amount of money? |
|---|---|---|---|---|---|
| | .58 | 1 | 1.7* | 137* | |
| | 58* | 100 | 170* | 14,000* | |
| | 100* | 169* | 290* | 23,153* | |
| Omri's Money | | | | | |

*These answers will vary according to the fluctuation of money values.

**The Lion, the Witch and the Wardrobe**
Project 11 Math:  Spring, March 20; Summer, June 21; Fall, September 23; Winter, December, 21
(These dates will vary by one day according to what calendar year you are looking up.)

**The Secret Garden**
Project 7 Math:

| Name of Person | Where Mary Met the Person | What Does the Person Do |
|---|---|---|
| Stationmaster | Thwaite Station | Stationmaster |
| Footman | Thwaite | Footman/carriage driver |
| Mr. Pitcher | Misselthwaite Manor | Manservant |
| Martha | Mary's bedroom | Housemaid |
| Ben Weatherstaff | Kitchen garden | Gardener |
| Dickon | Under tree in garden | Friend |
| Mr. Craven | A room at Misselthwaite Manor | Mary's uncle |
| Colin | Colin's bedroom | Mary's cousin |
| Dr. Craven | Colin's bedroom | Colin's doctor |
| Nurse | Colin's bedroom | Colin's nurse |

GA1425

**Where the Red Fern Grows**
Project 8 Math:    38 raccoons

**From the Mixed-Up Files of Mrs. Basil E. Frankweiler**
Project 1 Physical Challenge:   24 possibilities in all
                                4 possibilities if Jane and Kevin always sit
                                next to a window

**Danny, the Champion of the World**
Project 4 Math:    60 mph = 2 miles in 2 minutes
                   30 mph = 1 mile in 2 minutes
                   10 mph = 10 miles in 60 minutes
                   60 mph = 20 miles in 20 minutes
                   30 mph = 15 miles in 30 minutes
                   30 mph = 20 miles in 40 minutes
                   60 mph = 30 miles in 30 minutes

| | |
|---|---|
| cheetah | 70 mph |
| lion | 50 mph |
| coyote | 43 mph |
| rabbit | 35 mph |
| grizzly bear | 30 mph |
| human | 27 mph |
| pig | 11 mph |
| spider | 1 mph |

**Sing Down the Moon**
Project 12 Math:   10 sheep the first year
                   14 sheep at the end of two years

**Johnny Tremain**
Project 11 Math:   1200 men
                   1140 muskets
                   7200 buttons
                   480 horseshoes

GA1425

# The Secret of the Indian
### by Lynne Reid Banks

**Chapters 1-2** — DRAMA

**Chapter 3** — £ one pound ≈ $ $1.68 — MATH

**Chapter 4** — SCIENCE

**Chapter 5** — Yee-Ha! — PHYSICAL CHALLENGE

**Chapters 6-8** — WRITING

**Chapter 9** — THE SECRET of the INDIAN — READING

**Chapters 10-11** — TEXAS, GREAT BRITAIN — SOCIAL STUDIES

**Chapter 12** — brill, pouffe, nicking, wheedled — LANGUAGE

**Chapter 13** — COOKING

**Chapter 14** — ART

**Chapters 15-16** — ABC — HANDWRITING

**Chapter 17-Epilogue** — MUSIC

Group Members

Credits

GA1425

# The Lion, the Witch and the Wardrobe

*by C.S. Lewis*

**Group Members**

_____
_____
_____
_____
_____
_____

| Chapter 1 | Chapters 2-3 | Chapter 4 |
|---|---|---|
| ART | SOCIAL STUDIES | COOKING |
| **Chapters 5-6** | **Chapters 7-8** | **Chapter 9** |
| PHYSICAL CHALLENGE | HANDWRITING | MUSIC |
| **Chapter 10** | **Chapter 11** | **Chapter 12** |
| READING | Spring Summer 365 Fall Winter — MATH | WRITING |
| **Chapter 13** | **Chapters 14-16** | **Chapter 17** |
| Son of Earth Son of Adam Emperor-Beyond-the-Sea Deep Magic — LANGUAGE | DRAMA | SCIENCE |

Credits

GA1425

Mrs. Frisby and the Rats of NIMH
by Robert C. O'Brien

Group Members

Credits

Chapters 8-9 — DRAMA
Chapters 10-12 — LANGUAGE
Chapters 13-14 — MUSIC
Chapters 6-7 — READING
Chapters 15-16 — SCIENCE
Chapters 3-5 — HANDWRITING
Chapters 17-19 — SOCIAL STUDIES
Chapters 1-2 — COOKING
Chapters 20-22 — ART
Chapters 27-28 — MATH
Chapters 25-26 — WRITING
Chapters 23-24 — PHYSICAL CHALLENGE

18

GA1425

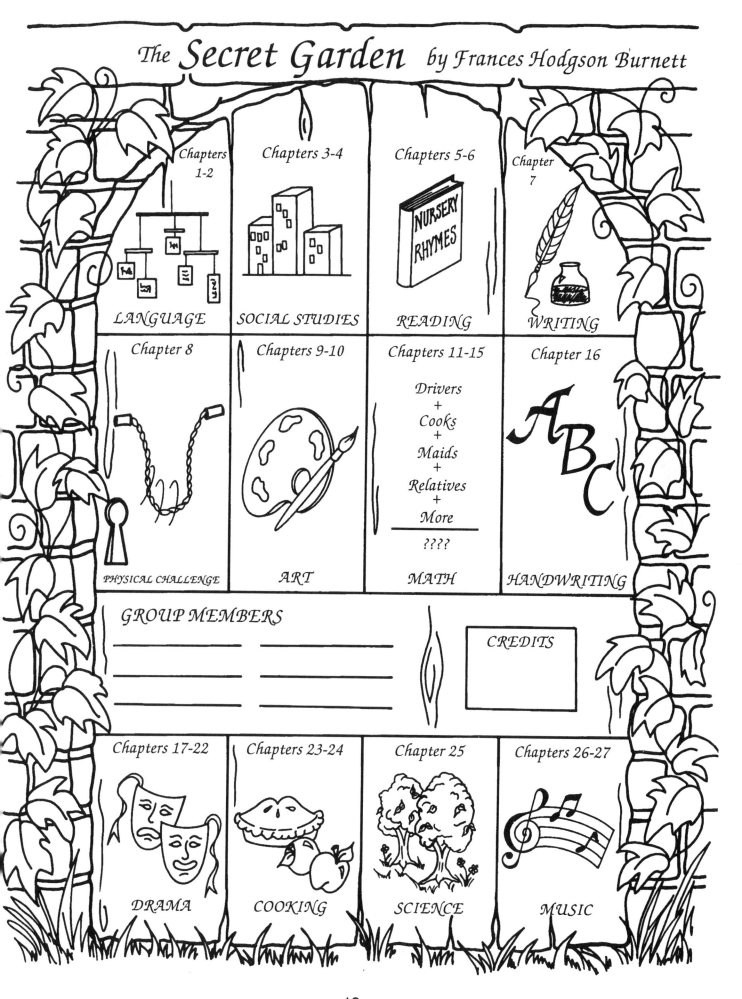

# The *Secret Garden* by Frances Hodgson Burnett

**Chapters 1-2** — LANGUAGE

**Chapters 3-4** — SOCIAL STUDIES

**Chapters 5-6** — READING

NURSERY RHYMES

**Chapter 7** — WRITING

**Chapter 8** — PHYSICAL CHALLENGE

**Chapters 9-10** — ART

**Chapters 11-15** — MATH

Drivers
+
Cooks
+
Maids
+
Relatives
+
More
————
????

**Chapter 16** — HANDWRITING

A
B
C

GROUP MEMBERS
_____  _____
_____  _____
_____  _____

CREDITS

**Chapters 17-22** — DRAMA

**Chapters 23-24** — COOKING

**Chapter 25** — SCIENCE

**Chapters 26-27** — MUSIC

GA1425

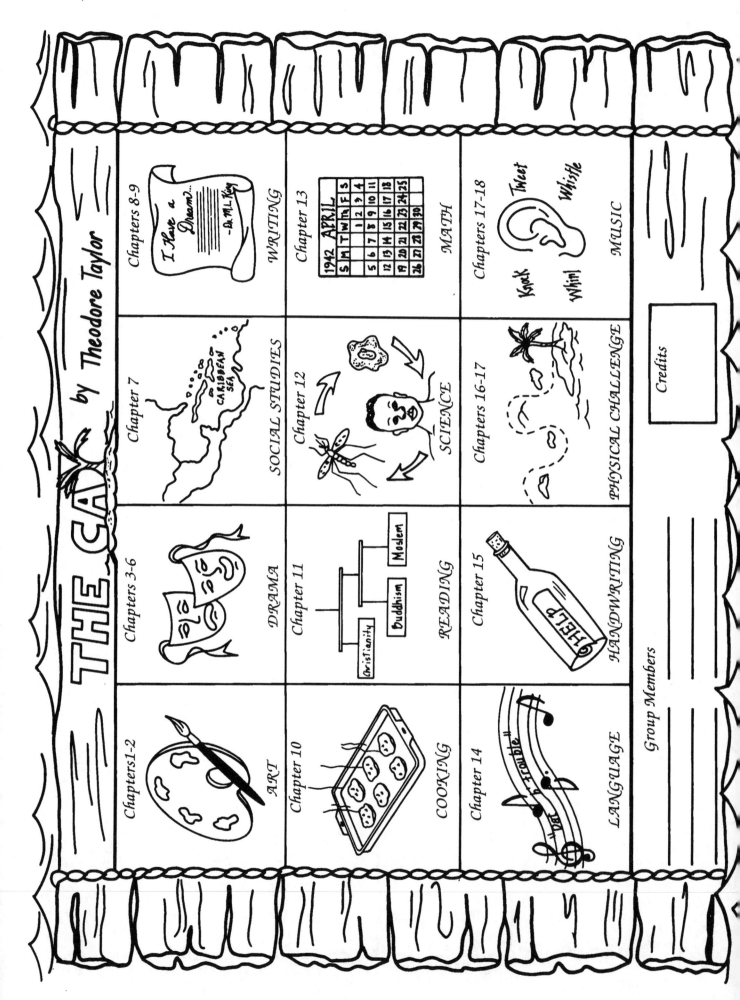

THE CAY by Theodore Taylor

Chapters 1-2 — ART
Chapters 3-6 — DRAMA
Chapter 7 — SOCIAL STUDIES
Chapters 8-9 — WRITING

Chapter 10 — COOKING
Chapter 11 — READING
Chapter 12 — SCIENCE
Chapter 13 — MATH

Chapter 14 — LANGUAGE
Chapter 15 — HANDWRITING
Chapters 16-17 — PHYSICAL CHALLENGE
Chapters 17-18 — MUSIC

1942 APRIL

Christianity  Buddhism  Moslem

HELP

Group Members

Credits

GA1425

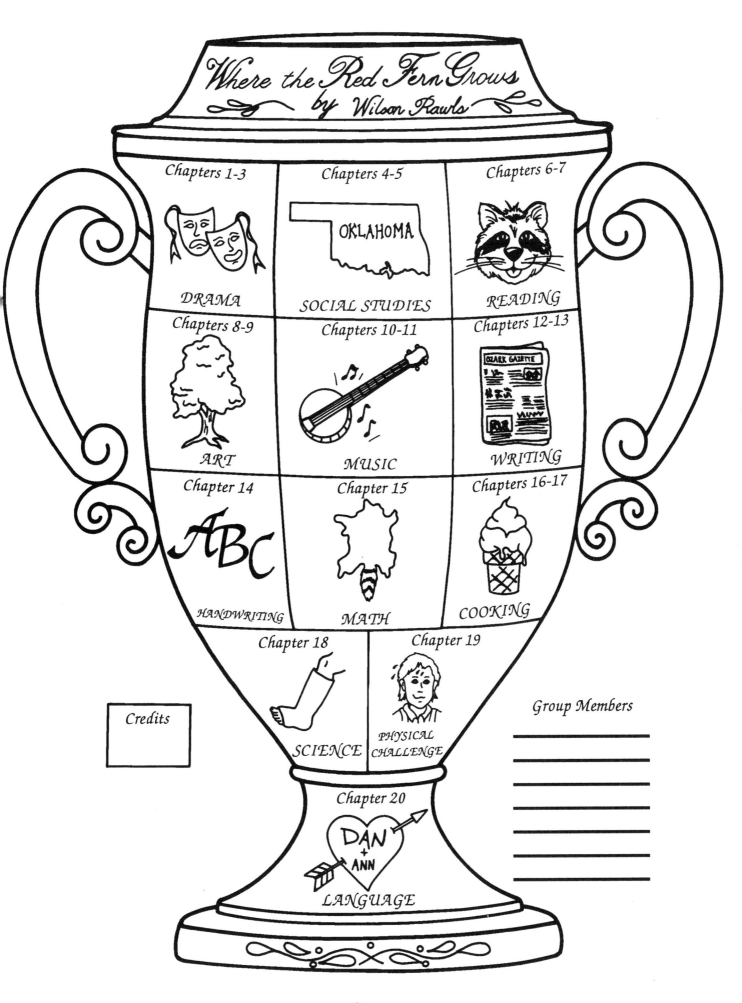

Where the Red Fern Grows
by Wilson Rawls

Chapters 1-3 — DRAMA

Chapters 4-5 — OKLAHOMA — SOCIAL STUDIES

Chapters 6-7 — READING

Chapters 8-9 — ART

Chapters 10-11 — MUSIC

Chapters 12-13 — OZARK GAZETTE — WRITING

Chapter 14 — ABC — HANDWRITING

Chapter 15 — MATH

Chapters 16-17 — COOKING

Chapter 18 — SCIENCE

Chapter 19 — PHYSICAL CHALLENGE

Credits

Group Members

Chapter 20 — DAN + ANN — LANGUAGE

GA1425

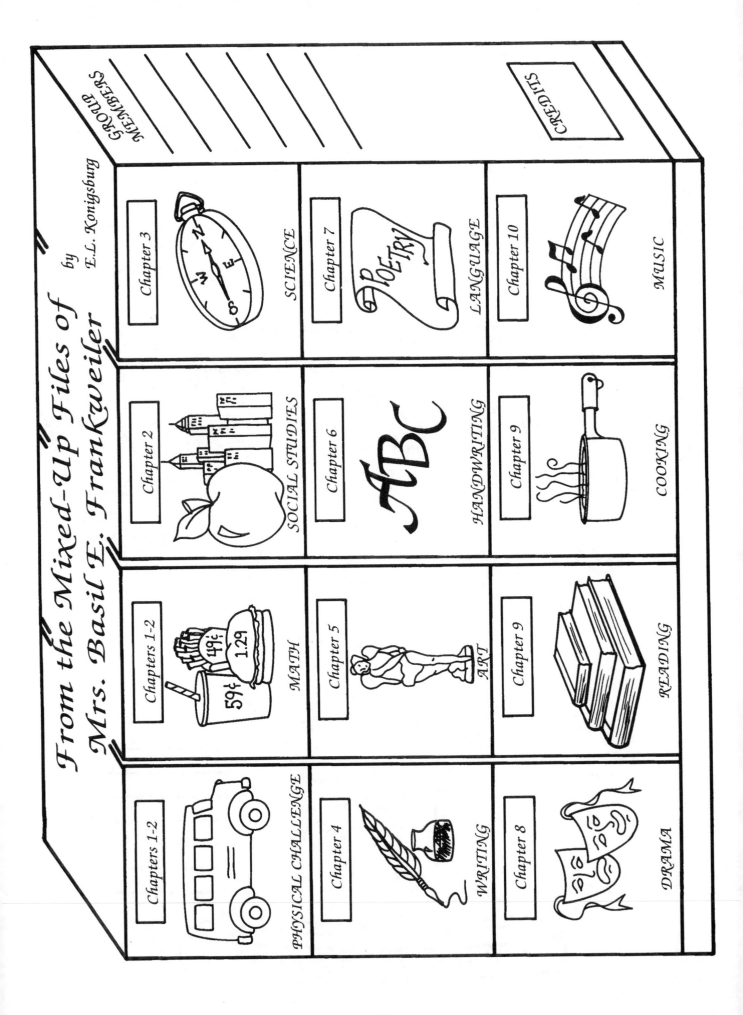

From the Mixed-Up Files of
Mrs. Basil E. Frankweiler

by E.L. Konigsburg

GROUP MEMBERS

CREDITS

Chapter 3
SCIENCE

Chapter 2
SOCIAL STUDIES

Chapters 1-2
MATH

Chapters 1-2
PHYSICAL CHALLENGE

Chapter 7
LANGUAGE

Chapter 6
HANDWRITING

Chapter 5
ART

Chapter 4
WRITING

Chapter 10
MUSIC

Chapter 9
COOKING

Chapter 9
READING

Chapter 8
DRAMA

GA1425

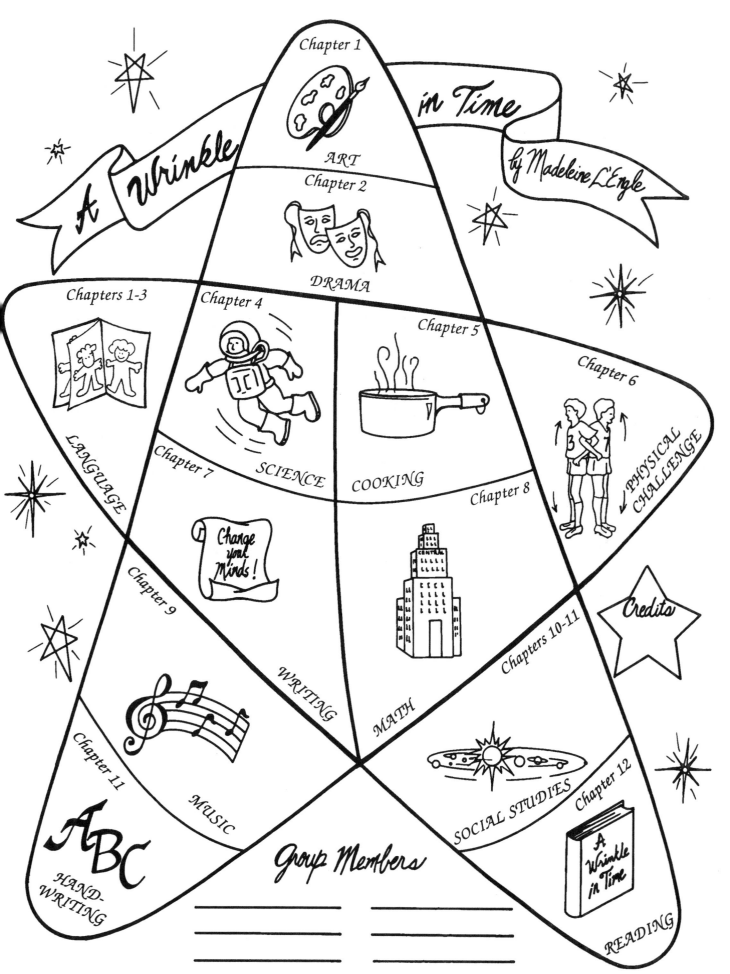

A Wrinkle in Time
by Madeleine L'Engle

Chapter 1 — ART

Chapter 2 — DRAMA

Chapters 1-3 — LANGUAGE

Chapter 4 — SCIENCE

Chapter 5 — COOKING

Chapter 6 — PHYSICAL CHALLENGE

Chapter 7 — Change your Minds! — WRITING

Chapter 8 — CENTRAL — MATH

Chapters 10-11 — SOCIAL STUDIES

Credits

Chapter 9 — MUSIC

Chapter 11 — ABC — HANDWRITING

Chapter 12 — A Wrinkle in Time — READING

Group Members
_____  _____
_____  _____

23

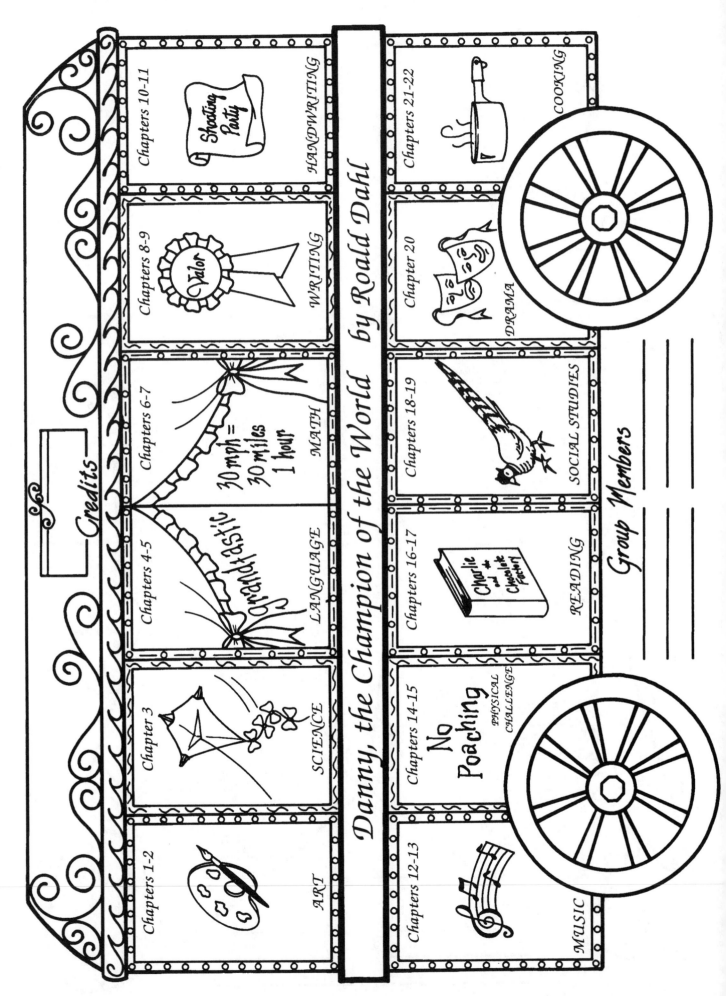

Danny, the Champion of the World  by Roald Dahl

Chapters 10-11 — Shooting Party — HANDWRITING

Chapters 8-9 — Valor — WRITING

Chapters 6-7 — 30 mph = 30 miles 1 hour — MATH

Chapters 4-5 — grandtastic — LANGUAGE

Chapter 3 — SCIENCE

Chapters 1-2 — ART

Chapters 21-22 — COOKING

Chapter 20 — DRAMA

Chapters 18-19 — SOCIAL STUDIES

Chapters 16-17 — Charlie and the Chocolate Factory — READING

Chapters 14-15 — No Poaching — PHYSICAL CHALLENGE

Chapters 12-13 — MUSIC

Credits

Group Members

GA1425

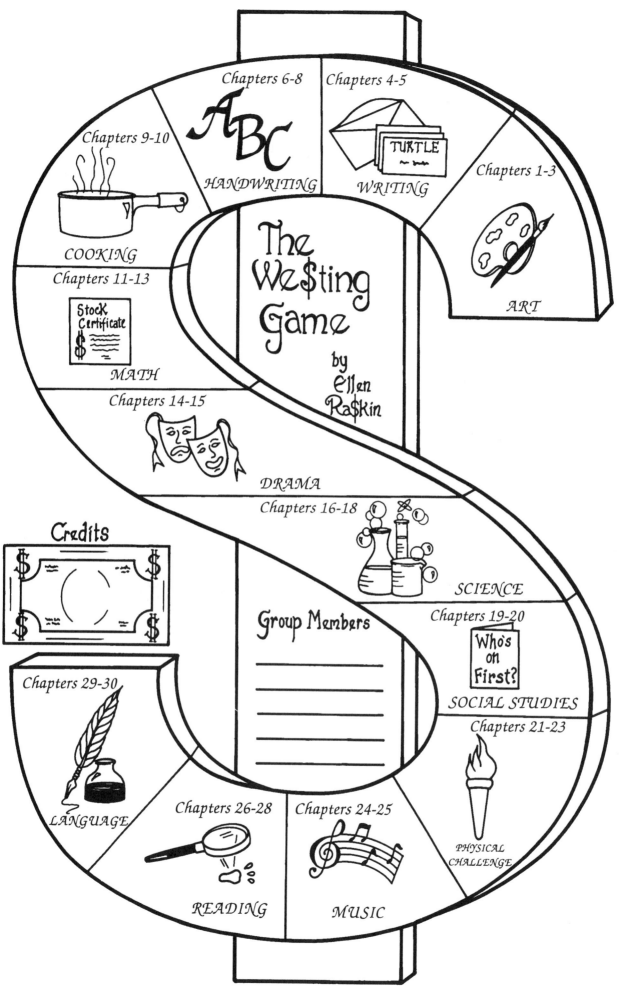

The We$ting Game

by Ellen Ra$kin

Chapters 6-8 — HANDWRITING

Chapters 4-5 — WRITING

Chapters 1-3 — ART

Chapters 9-10 — COOKING

Chapters 11-13 — MATH

Chapters 14-15 — DRAMA

Chapters 16-18 — SCIENCE

Chapters 19-20 — SOCIAL STUDIES

Chapters 21-23 — PHYSICAL CHALLENGE

Chapters 24-25 — MUSIC

Chapters 26-28 — READING

Chapters 29-30 — LANGUAGE

Credits

Group Members

GA1425

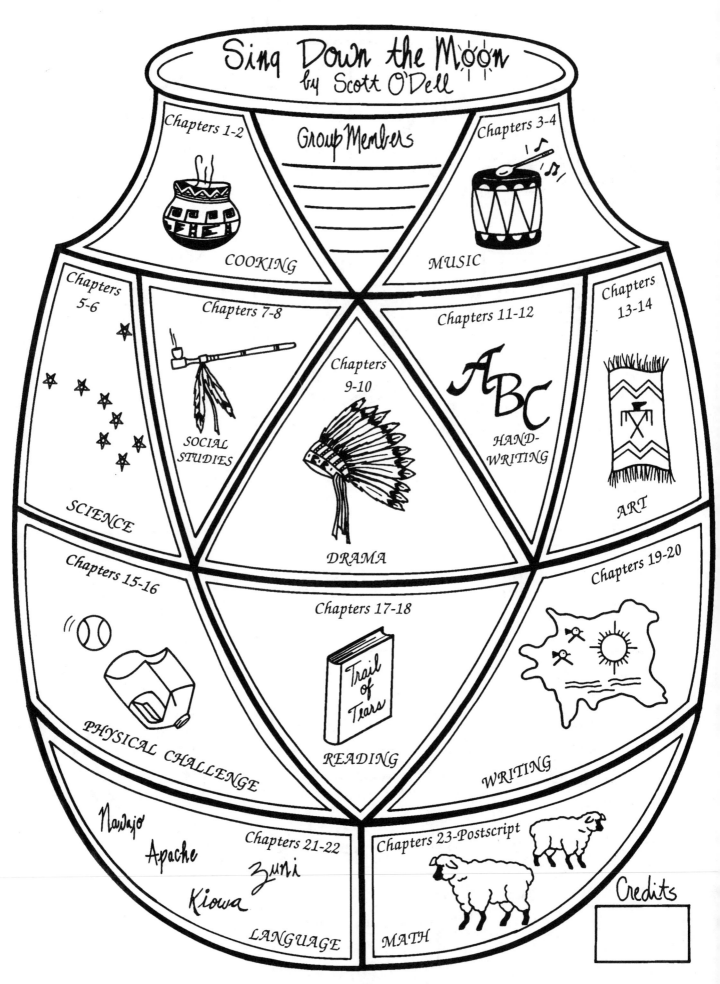

Sing Down the Moon
by Scott O'Dell

Chapters 1-2 — COOKING

Group Members

Chapters 3-4 — MUSIC

Chapters 5-6 — SCIENCE

Chapters 7-8 — SOCIAL STUDIES

Chapters 9-10 — DRAMA

Chapters 11-12 — HAND-WRITING

Chapters 13-14 — ART

Chapters 15-16 — PHYSICAL CHALLENGE

Chapters 17-18 — READING

Chapters 19-20 — WRITING

Chapters 21-22 — LANGUAGE

Navajo Apache Zuni Kiowa

Chapters 23-Postscript — MATH

Credits

GA1425

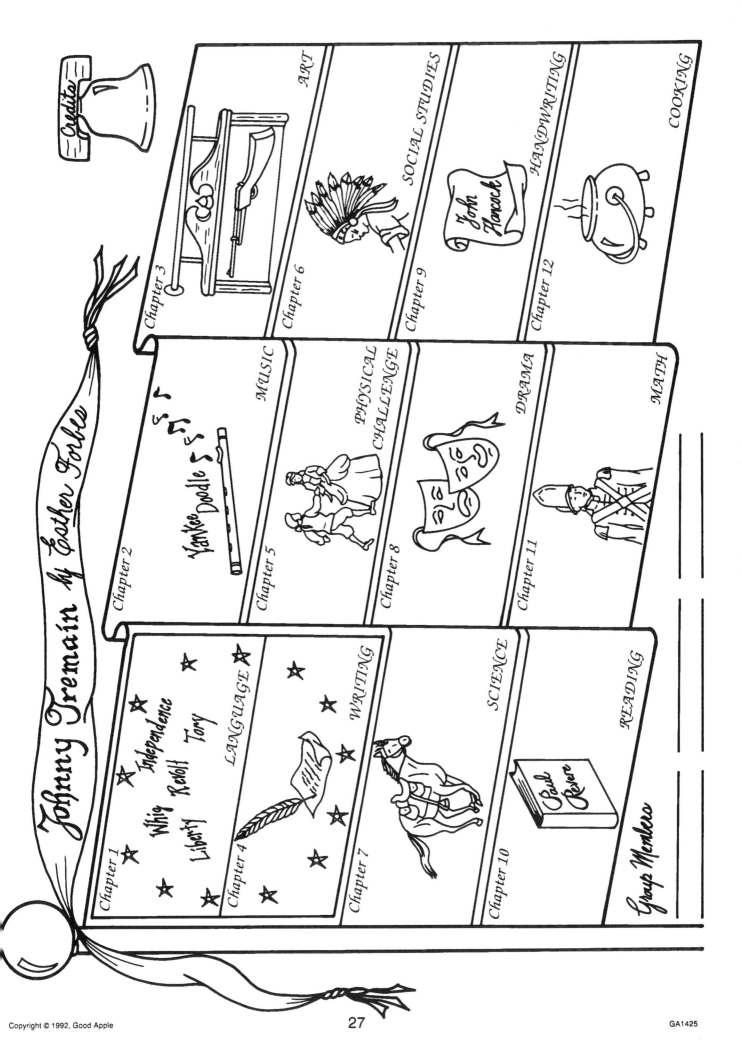

Johnny Tremain by Esther Forbes

**Chapter 1** — LANGUAGE — Independence, Whig, Liberty, Revolt, Tory

**Chapter 2** — MUSIC — Yankee Doodle

**Chapter 3** — ART

**Chapter 4** — WRITING

**Chapter 5** — PHYSICAL CHALLENGE

**Chapter 6** — SOCIAL STUDIES

**Chapter 7** — SCIENCE

**Chapter 8** — DRAMA

**Chapter 9** — HANDWRITING — John Hancock

**Chapter 10** — READING — Paul Revere

**Chapter 11** — MATH

**Chapter 12** — COOKING

Credits

Group Members _____

GA1425

# The Secret of the Indian
## by Lynne Reid Banks

Chapter 1: Shocking Homecoming　　　　　　　Project 1: Drama
Chapter 2: Modest Heroes

What a way to start a book! The first two chapters of *The Secret of the Indian* do start out with a bang.

Compose a short skit that shows the "chaos after the fact." Start your skit as Omri's parents come in the house. You should have some makeup for Omri's burned face. The four main characters in these two chapters should be incorporated with minor characters being written into the play if you have enough actors. Present the play to your class.

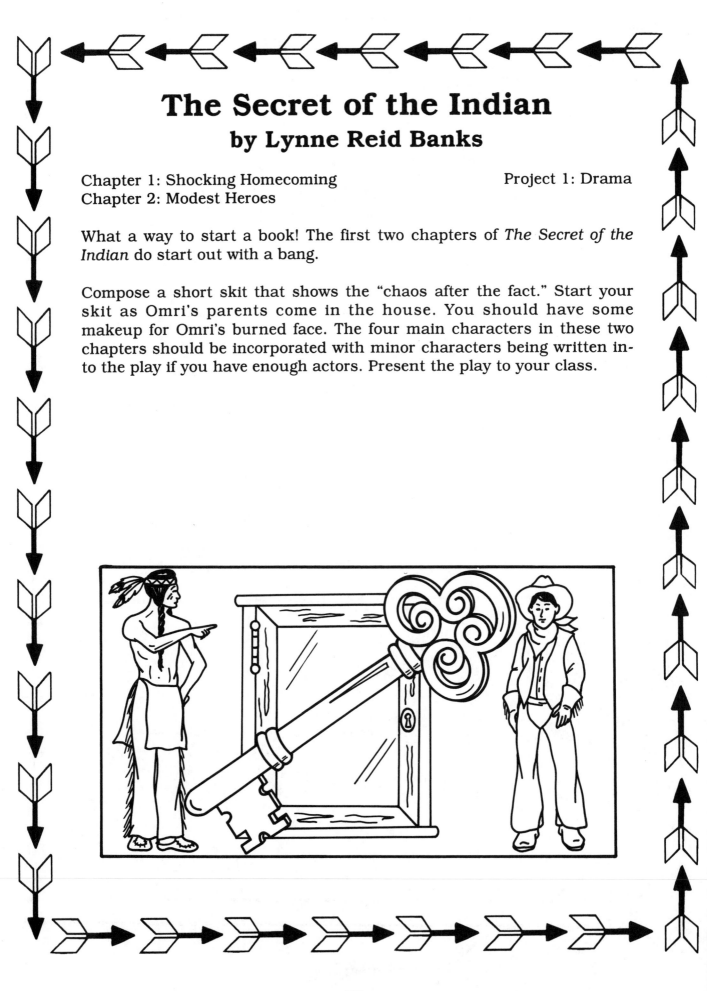

GA1425

# The Secret of the Indian
## by Lynne Reid Banks

Chapter 3: How It All Started

Project 2: Math

Omri's story, "The Plastic Indian," was truly a prize-winning work of literature. Omri's prize of three hundred pounds impressed his brother, but how much was it worth in dollars? Check the financial section of your newspaper, call a travel agency or library, and calculate the rate of exchange to fill in the chart below.

| Pounds | Dollars | German Marks | Japenese Yen | What could you purchase with this amount of money? |
|---|---|---|---|---|
| | 1 | | | |
| | 100 | | | |
| 100 | | | | |
| | | | | |

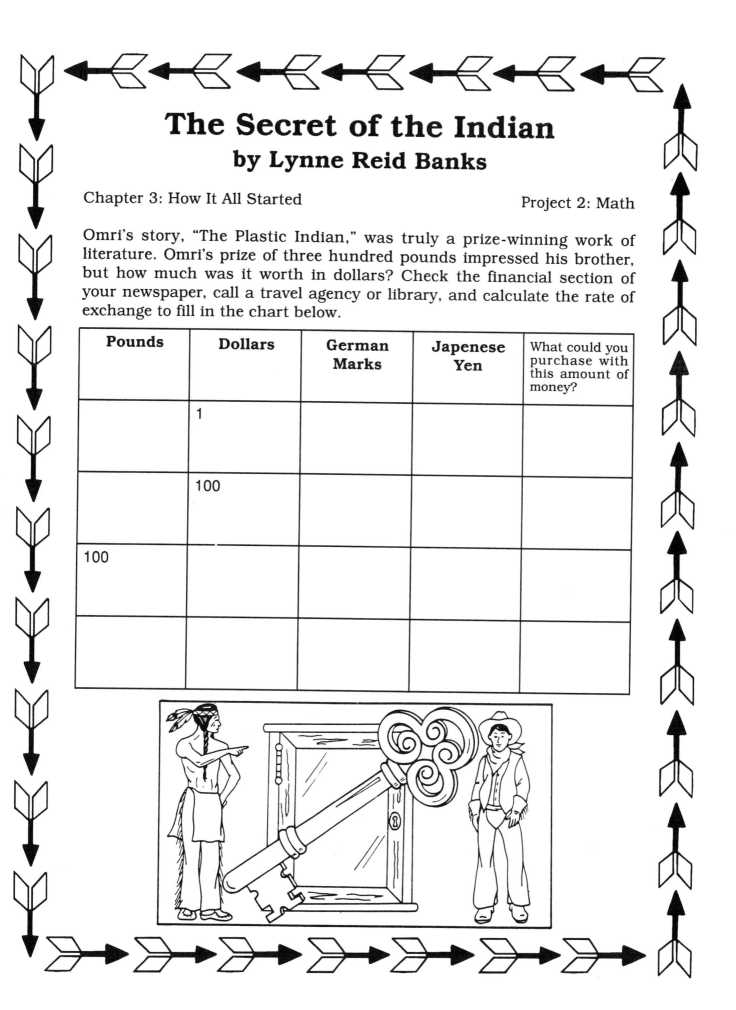

GA1425

# The Secret of the Indian
## by Lynne Reid Banks

Chapter 4: Dead in the Night                    Project 3: Science

Make an instant replay of how your team envisions bringing a plastic figure to life. Make a time warp machine like in the book. The project must show:

1. the plastic figure
2. the plastic figure in the transfer to real-life stage
3. the changed real-life stage

Make it really scientific. Post the scientific discovery on the bulletin board.

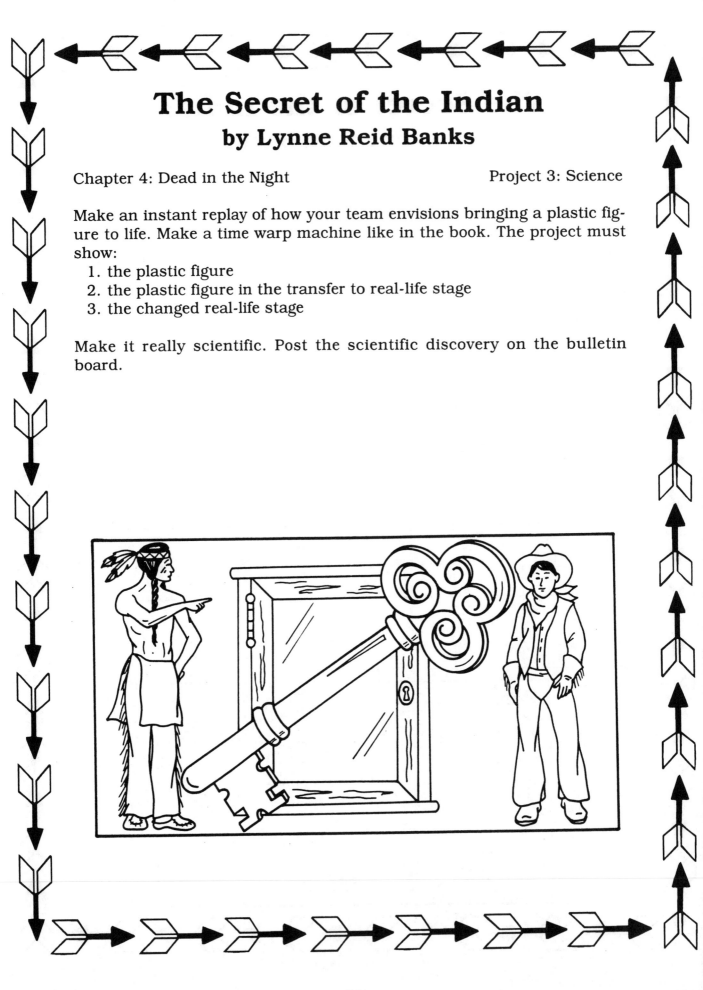

GA1425

# The Secret of the Indian
## by Lynne Reid Banks

Chapter 5: Patrick Goes Back          Project 4: Physical Challenge

It's Western Roundup Day, Yee-Ha!
Turn your classroom into a rodeo by organizing three different rodeo competitions.

a. Lasso a steer (Use a chair for the steer.)
b. Team barrel races (Use baseball bats or broomsticks as horses; set up chairs as the barrels.)
c. Three-legged race (Use jump ropes or yarn to tie your legs; you will need a partner.)

Be creative and add other events.

On your mark, get set, go!

GA1425

# The Secret of the Indian
## by Lynne Reid Banks

Chapter 6: A New Insider
Chapter 7: Patrick in Boone-Land
Chapter 8: A Heart Stops Beating

Project 5: Writing

Real live people, living animals only three inches (7.62 cm) tall. Can it be? How will the insects and other small creatures take this?

Write a group paper from an ant's point of view about humans' new size. Tell how the ant colony will cope with human beings that are the same size as they are. The ants could rule the earth! The ants must have an opinion on this major twist in their environment. Help them speak their minds. Post your group paper on the bulletin board.

GA1425

# The Secret of the Indian
## by Lynne Reid Banks

Chapter 9: Tamsin Drives a Bargain  Project 6: Reading

Read out loud an excerpt from Chapter 9 to the rest of the class. If your team chooses, everyone can read a few sentences. Read just enough to get the rest of the class interested and hooked on the book.

Whoever reads the Matron part should have a nurse's hat. Think of hats that would represent the other characters that will speak in the excerpt that you have chosen. Be ready to answer questions about the cupboard, the medical team, Boone and more. You will be good promoters of the book.

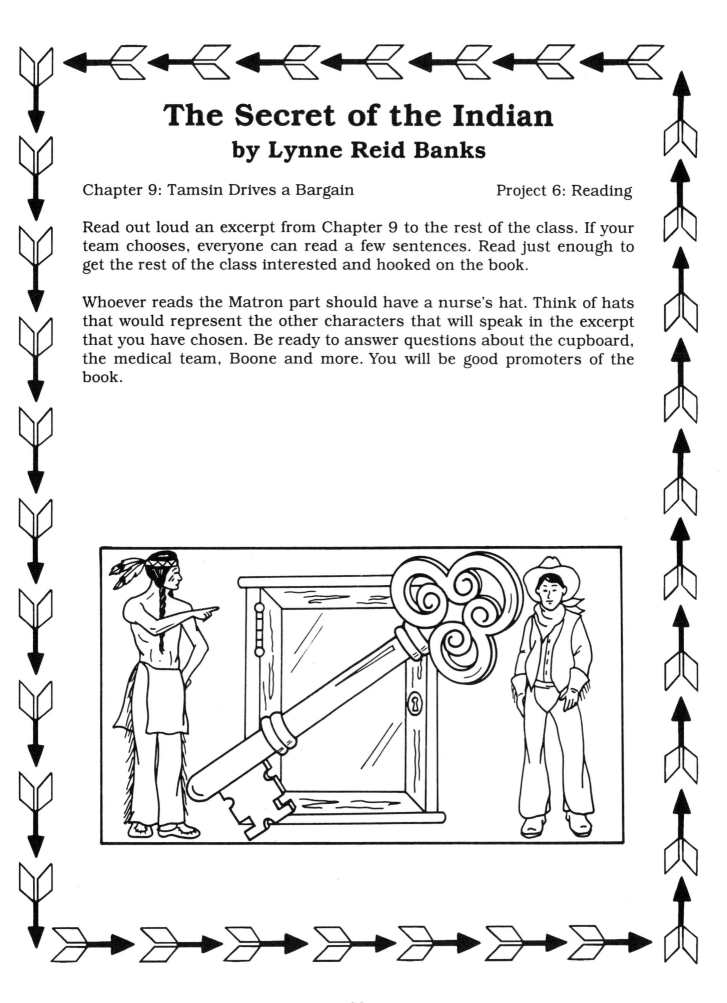

33

GA1425

# The Secret of the Indian
## by Lynne Reid Banks

Chapter 10: A Rough Ride
Chapter 11: Ruby Lou

Project 7: Social Studies

Howdy, Partner! Tell me what you know about the lay of the land. That is, the land in Texas and the land in England. Make a map of Texas and a map of England to show geographic likenesses and differences.

Use whatever medium you would like. Present your maps to the class and post them in the room.

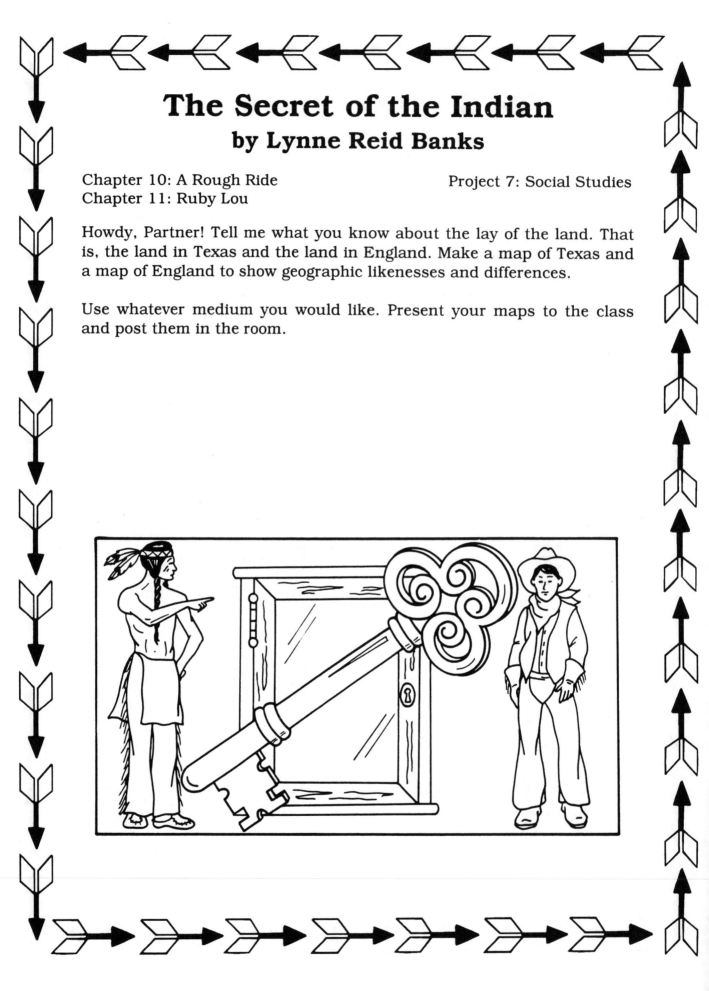

GA1425

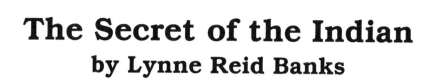

# The Secret of the Indian
## by Lynne Reid Banks

Chapter 12: Caught Red-Handed                    Project 8: Language

Dialects and slang are different even if you travel within a small area. People make up their own words to fit the situation and sometimes those made-up words stick around for a long time. As you look back through the previous chapters, your team will get a flavor for the English and Texan dialects. The following list of words is found in the book. Give what your team thinks as their meanings. Make a sentence with each word. (Don't use the sentence from the book.)

Chapter 1:    daft, nipped
Chapter 4:    nicking
Chapter 6:    brill
Chapter 9:    pouffe
Chapter 11:   wheedled
Chapter 12:   sidled

Post the words and sentences in the room.

                    GA1425

# The Secret of the Indian
## by Lynne Reid Banks

Chapter 13: Mr. Johnson Smells a Rat                    Project 9: Cooking

Mr. Johnson thinks he knows what he thought he saw a year ago when Patrick and Omri were in his office, and is he angry, confused and out to tell someone. In other words, he smells a rat. The only way to stop him is through his stomach and the smell of food. He is fond of cookies. But the only stipulation he has is that they have to be homemade.

Get with it, team, and bake "Mr. Johnson" (alias, your very own principal) a batch of cookies. You never know; you may make some points with the principal.

Save a cookie for your teacher, since your credit points come from this person!

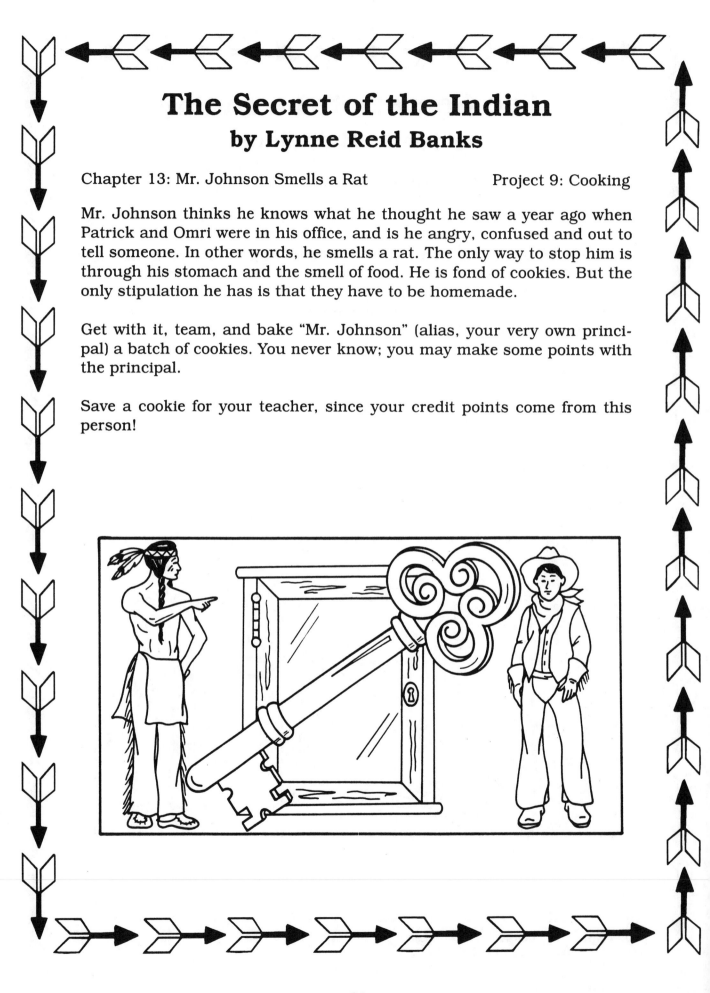

GA1425

# The Secret of the Indian
## by Lynne Reid Banks

Chapter 14: A Strange Yellow Sky

Project 10: Art

Patrick is experiencing new sounds and smells while Ruby Lou is concerned about the color of the sky. Make an illustration of one of the "sensational" scenes in Chapter 14. The operative word is *senses*.

Pick a scene that shows Patrick experiencing new sights, smells, sounds or tastes. There are quite a few to choose from. As your team considers the project, think about drawing tools that you have not yet used. Make this project unique.

Post your illustration.

GA1425

# The Secret of the Indian
## by Lynne Reid Banks

Chapter 15: Interrogation
Chapter 16: Panic

Project 11: Handwriting

The cookies you made in Chapter 13 did not prevent Mr. Johnson from breaking down. He is ready to make a statement about the "Red Indian" he saw about a year ago.

Your team must take on the role of Mr. Johnson and run to the press with the unbelievable news that you have finally substantiated that there is in fact a live miniature Indian living in the pocket of a young man.

Your team, as Mr. Johnson, must submit a handwritten statement to the police and the news media. The handwritten information must show a sturdy, stable, mature flair that the media will believe. Your media contact is your teacher. Post the headline in the room.

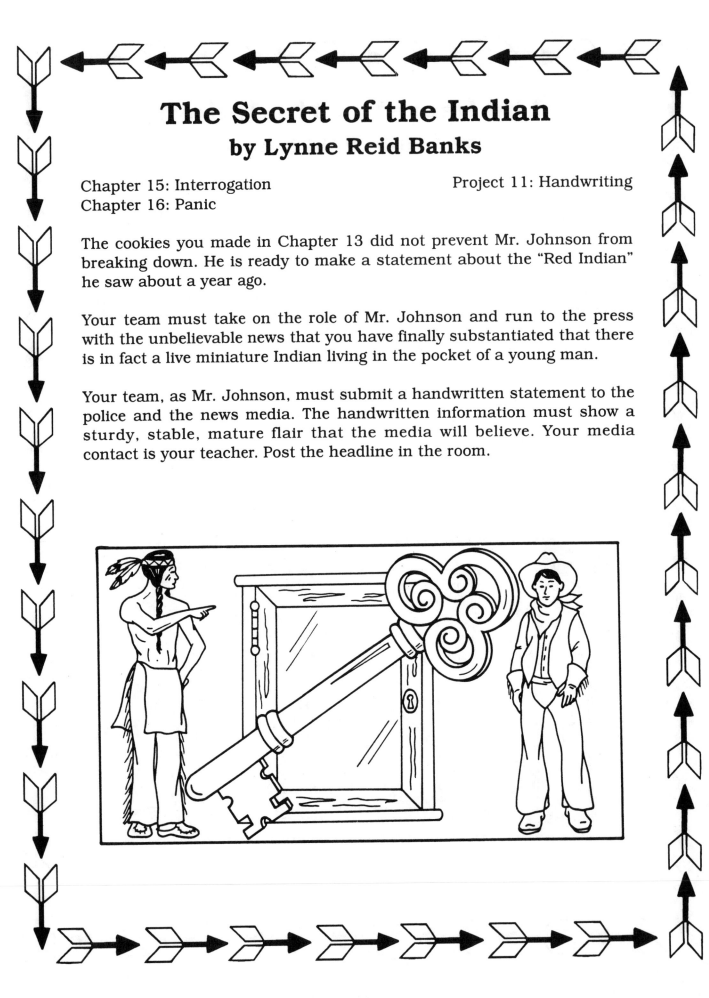

GA1425

# The Secret of the Indian
## by Lynne Reid Banks

Chapter 17: The Big Blow
Chapter 18: Red Satin
Epilogue: At the Wedding

Project 12: Music

The climax for this book can best be explained through music and verse. The violence and noise of the natural disaster and the destruction should be incorporated into the song to start it off nice and loud. A soft interlude that tells the next part of the story should follow. And as your team reads the epilogue, the wedding song will come to mind. Make your classy song tell it all.

Your team can use familiar songs but change the words.

Perform your wonderful creation for the class.

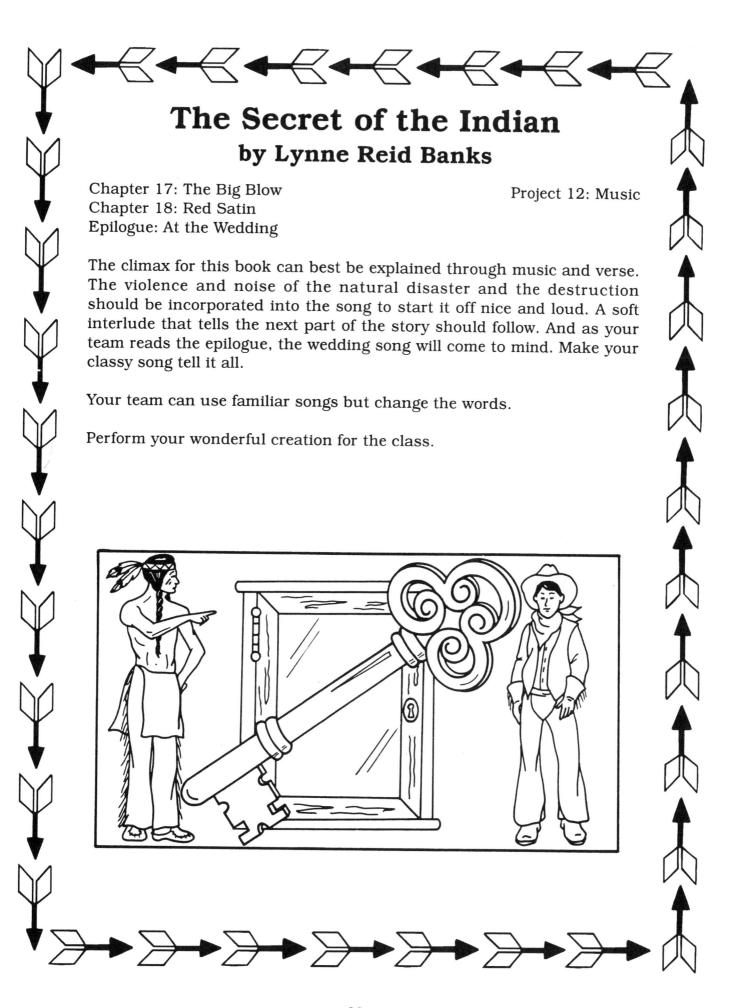

GA1425

# The Lion, the Witch and the Wardrobe

## by C.S. Lewis

Chapter 1: Lucy Looks into a Wardrobe                    Project 1: Art

It was customary to send children away from London during World War II because of the air bombings. The four children of this story were no different. They were lucky enough to be sent to an old professor's house that was filled with history and adventure.

The first chapter exposes the "adventure capsule." Your team must figure out what is the adventure capsule and make a replica of it.

Make it three dimensional so you can see inside of it.

GA1425

# The Lion, the Witch and the Wardrobe
## by C.S. Lewis

Chapter 2: What Lucy Found There       Project 2: Social Studies
Chapter 3: Edmund and the Wardrobe

In Chapters 2 and 3, two of the children take a trip into the wardrobe and travel to an unbelievable place outside the world we know. Let's send them on another trip.

Designate two of your team members to be Lucy and Edmund. They will think of a place to visit in our real world, like a national park, or city, historical spot, special place in your community, etc. The rest of the team will ask them twenty yes and no questions and hopefully guess the place of which they are thinking.

On a broader scale, your team can have a place in mind and the rest of the class can ask twenty questions.

GA1425

# The Lion, the Witch and the Wardrobe
## by C.S. Lewis

Chapter 4: Turkish Delight                    Project 3: Cooking

As you read Chapter 4 the food that is described sounds pretty tasty. Your team can cash in on a new restaurant idea: sandwiches from Narnia, a far out Deli.

This innovative restaurant does not use worldly monies for payment, so your team must think of an alternate way of paying. (There are a lot of ways to pay in the classroom setting: trade-off skills, talents, credits, tutoring time, and many more that you will think of that will work.)

Your team can bring to class "fixings" for sandwiches (use crackers instead of bread) and of course, give the sandwiches new unique names. Set up a new wave deli and see what it takes to be an entrepreneur.

GA1425

# The Lion, the Witch and the Wardrobe
## by C.S. Lewis

Chapter 5: Back on This Side of the Door    Project 4: Physical Challenge
Chapter 6: Into the Forest

A game of Hide and Seek was in progress as the children took their trip in the wardrobe. It may sound silly, but your team's mission is to take the basic game of Hide and Seek and turn it into a game that your whole class can play.

Give the game a new name but keep the rules about the same. You can incorporate some of the things that Lucy and Edmund saw in Narnia. Good luck!

GA1425

# The Lion, the Witch and the Wardrobe
## by C.S. Lewis

Chapter 7: A Day with the Beavers

Chapter 8: What Happened After Dinner

Project 5: Handwriting

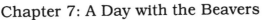

You and your family (team) are going to be moving to Narnia and want to find a house just like that of the beavers. You are looking for the same kind of location that the beavers have and are very set in having a house like the house that is described in Chapter 7.

One of the stipulations in applying for a house in Narnia is that you must write down your house desires and submit it to the real estate agent in your classroom (teacher). Oh, one more rule–your application must be written in calligraphy. Good house hunting!

GA1425

# The Lion, the Witch and the Wardrobe
## by C.S. Lewis

Chapter 9: In the Witch's House                          Project 6: Music

After reading Chapters 9 and 10 your team should have a good idea of what is going on at the Witch's Castle. With the information that you read, compose a winter melody that tells about the many statues in the Witch's courtyard.

The winter setting brings to mind many wonderful winter tunes that your team could use for the melody. Happy composing!  Present your composition to the class.

# The Lion, the Witch and the Wardrobe
## by C.S. Lewis

Chapter 10: The Spell Begins to Break                    Project 7: Reading

The three children and the beavers set out on a trip in the middle of a very cold spell over some difficult terrain. When they finally stop for the night, little Lucy wants a bedtime story read to her, but the beavers, not being from Lucy's world, did not know any bedtime stories.

Find a bedtime/fairy tale to read to Lucy. Pretend that the rest of the class is Lucy and read the story in unison to them. Turn the lights out and have the class put their heads on their desks for added creativity.

46

GA1425

# The Lion, the Witch and the Wardrobe
## by C.S. Lewis

Chapter 11: Aslan Is Nearer                                    Project 8: Math

Spring has sprung in Chapter 11, you may think. Don't get too excited because things can change drastically in Narnia. How many earth days are in each season: spring, summer, fall, winter?

What are the dates that each season begins? Post this seasonal information on the bulletin board.

GA1425

# The Lion, the Witch and the Wardrobe
## by C.S. Lewis

Chapter 12: Peter's First Battle                    Project 9: Writing

The characters of Narnia have been stifled for a long time. During these trying times the Dwarf for the White Witch was required to keep a log of everyday happenings. Deep down inside, the Dwarf wanted to express his feelings about the crisis that Narnia was in, but the Witch would have turned him to stone if she had found out.

Take a risk for the Dwarf and write a diary excerpt of Chapter 12 the way he would really have wanted to report the coming of spring.

P.S. It is promised the White Witch will not get her hands on the diary and turn you into stone! Post your diary excerpt on the bulletin board.

GA1425

# The Lion, the Witch and the Wardrobe
## by C.S. Lewis

Chapter 13: Deep Magic from the Dawn of Time          Project 10: Reading

Throughout the book, interesting terms and phrases appear to challenge our minds and linguistic interpretations. Here are a few for your team to interpret. Brainstorm among your team and write down the meaning of the following:  Son of Earth
Son of Adam
Emperor-Beyond-the-Sea
Deep Magic

Use each phrase in a sentence.

GA1425

# The Lion, the Witch and the Wardrobe
## by C.S. Lewis

Chapter 14: The Triumph of the Witch

Chapter 15: Deeper Magic Before the Dawn of Time

Chapter 16: What Happened About the Statues?

Project 11: Drama

What a dramatic turn in the story! Reenact Chapters 14,15 and 16 with puppets that your team makes. A few different materials that you might consider using for the puppets are paper bags, socks or paper plates.

GA1425

# The Lion, the Witch and the Wardrobe
## by C.S. Lewis

Chapter 17: The Hunting of the White Stag          Project 12: Science

The doors of the wardrobe are shut and can never be used again to get to Narnia. To keep the magic of Narnia forever, put together a list of scientific and fantasy words that will propel us back to Narnia. Roll up your recipe and put it in a glass bottle. Set it in the classroom where everyone can see it. Do not say anything about the bottle and see how many classmates pick it up or ask you about what is in the bottle.

GA1425

# Mrs. Frisby and the Rats of NIMH
## by Robert C. O'Brien

Chapter 1: The Sickness of Timothy Frisby
Chapter 2: Mr. Ages

Project 1: Cooking

Mrs. Frisby was happy to find the abandoned winter supply of food. Substituting popcorn for the corn, make a "trail mix" from the items described in the book. Have all team members bring in one of the items and allow them to include other "tasties" to make a yummy snack to share with the class.

GA1425

# Mrs. Frisby and the Rats of NIMH
## by Robert C. O'Brien

Chapter 3: The Crow and the Cat
Chapter 4: Mr. Fitzgibbon's Plow
Chapter 5: Five Days

Project 2: Handwriting

Jeremy and Mrs. Frisby have a narrow escape from the long claws and sharp fangs of Dragon, the cat. Create a poem that describes their narrow escape. Have all members of your group contribute to the poem. Use your best handwriting (calligraphy?) and post your poem for your class to see.

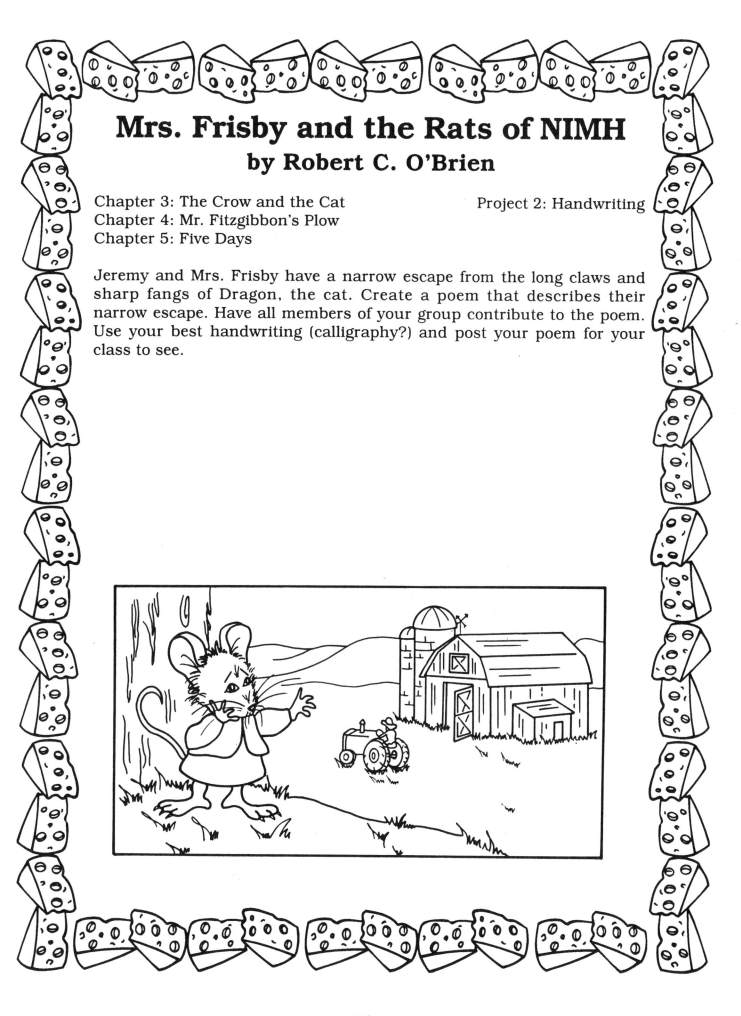

GA1425

# Mrs. Frisby and the Rats of NIMH
## by Robert C. O'Brien

Chapter 6: A Favor from Jeremy
Chapter 7: The Owl

Project 3: Reading

In *Mrs. Frisby and the Rats of NIMH* a mouse helps a crow, an owl helps a mouse, and rats end up helping solve Mrs. Frisby's problem. In *Charlotte's Web* a spider helps a pig with the aid of a rat. To refresh your memory, look through some of your favorite "animal" books from your younger storybook days and give examples of how animals of different kinds help each other. If the book is about a dog, for example, draw a dog shape and write your examples of helping each other on the animal shape. Display your work so classmates can enjoy it.

GA1425

# Mrs. Frisby and the Rats of NIMH
## by Robert C. O'Brien

Chapter 8: "Go to the Rats"                                   Project 4: Drama
Chapter 9: In the Rosebush

Beginning with the sentence, "'We're here,' Jeremy said in a low voice," create a readers' theater play about the encounter between Jeremy, Mrs. Frisby, and the owl.

Divide the section into four parts. Part one is a narrator's brief explanation to the listeners about the events leading up to the meeting. Part two is that of Jeremy, and parts three and four are Mrs. Frisby and the owl.

After writing the introduction, rehearse the section of the book to show Mrs. Frisby's fear and the owl's worldly and wise attitude. Practice the dialogue several times; then make a readers' theater presentation to the class.

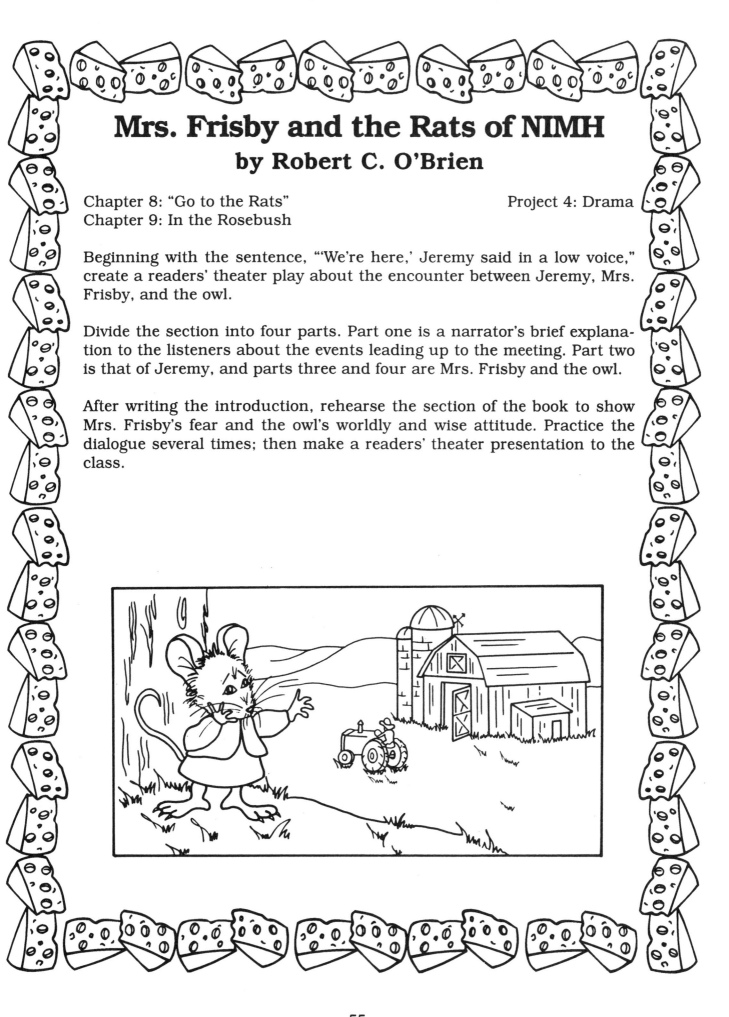

55

GA1425

# Mrs. Frisby and the Rats of NIMH
## by Robert C. O'Brien

Chapter 10: Brutus
Chapter 11: In the Library
Chapter 12: Isabella

Project 5: Language

Anthropomorphism is a novel technique to bring animals to life in a human way. For example, Timothy the mouse becomes human by wearing clothing, speaking, buying women's favors, etc. We sometimes talk to our pets as if they were human and could understand everything we say to them. Each member of your team is to write a short animal story using anthropomorphism. (What will it be...a seal...a snail...a dragon... or a...?) Share your stories with your classmates.

56

GA1425

# Mrs. Frisby and the Rats of NIMH
## by Robert C. O'Brien

Chapter 13: A Powder for Dragon
Chapter 14: The Marketplace

Project 6: Music

Pump up the volume!

Make a "mouse" radio broadcast complete with mouse music and mouse news. Be sure to include in your news a warning to all mice and rats about the abductions at the marketplace. How about a commercial for "cheese whisker cleaner" or "fur conditioner"? Use your imagination, have fun, and present your broadcast to your classmates.

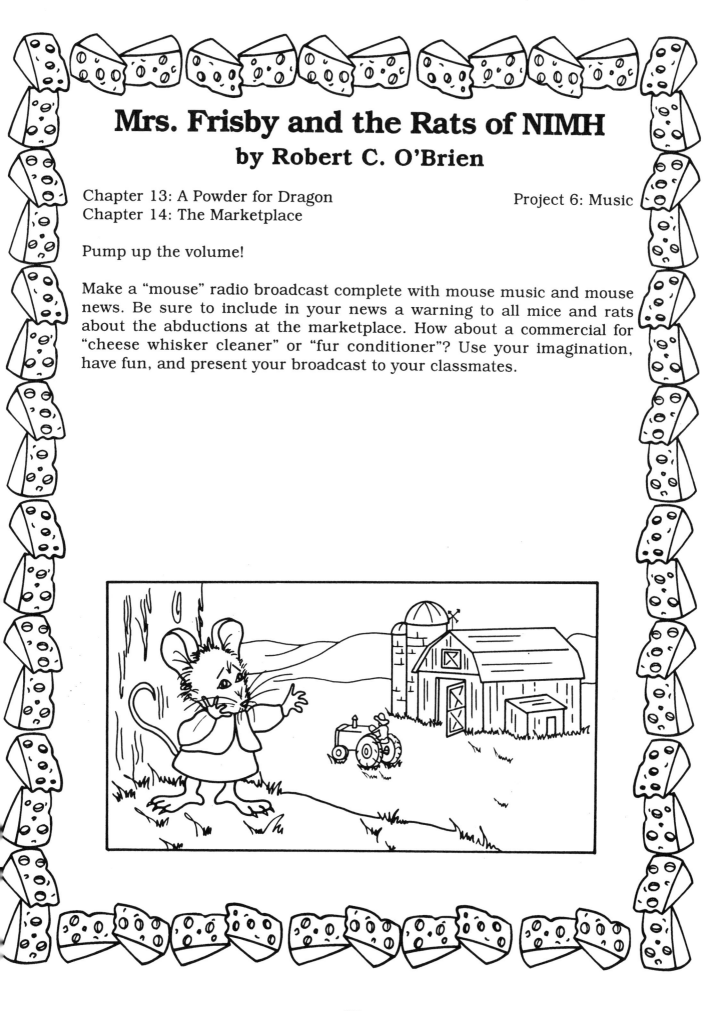

GA1425

# Mrs. Frisby and the Rats of NIMH
## by Robert C. O'Brien

Chapter 15: In the Cage
Chapter 16: The Maze

Project 7: Science

A learning curve is a graph that can show how long it takes to learn something. The more times you practice a task, the better or faster you can accomplish it.

Experiment with the learning curve idea. Each member of your team will make a "maze" on paper and duplicate eight copies. Have another member of your group "run" the maze eight times with a pencil and record the time it takes to complete each run. Make a graph or chart of the results and present the finished chart with interpretations about each person's learning curve.

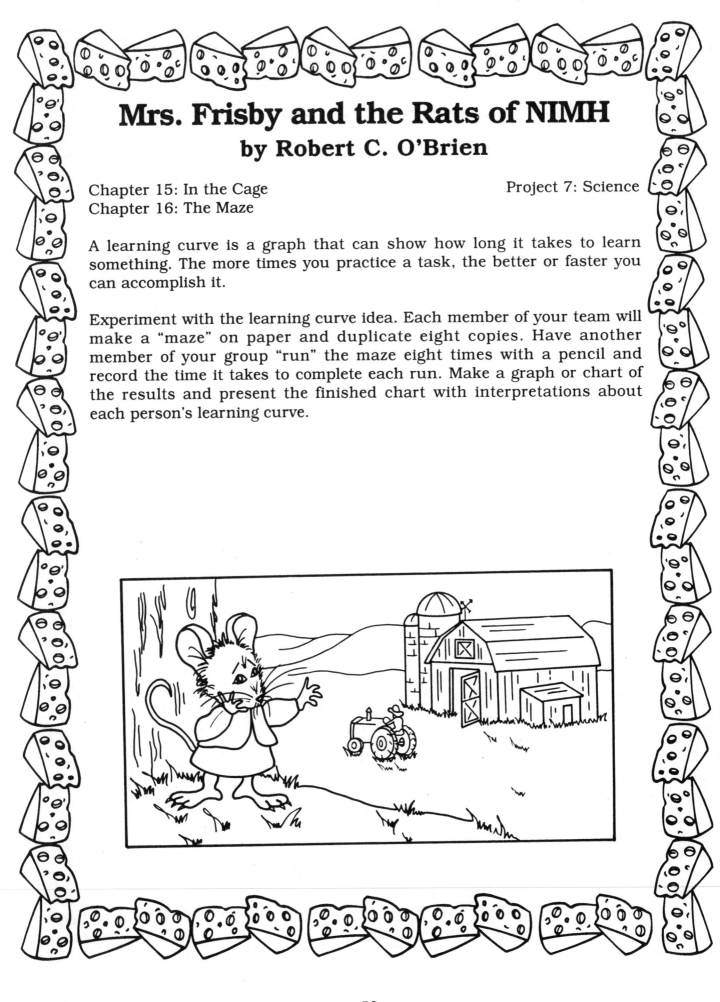

GA1425

# Mrs. Frisby and the Rats of NIMH
## by Robert C. O'Brien

Chapter 17: A Lesson in Reading
Chapter 18: The Air Ducts
Chapter 19: The Boniface Estate

Project 8: Social Studies

The rats of NIMH stayed at the Boniface Estates while Mr. Boniface was on a trip around the world. What a great adventure this could be! Your team has been turned into a travel agency and must plan an "around-the-world" travel tour. Include maps, brochures, and highlights to be seen while on this year-long adventure. Let each member plan a particular portion of the trip and present this hypothetical trip to the class with pictures, costs, brochures (you can make these yourselves), tickets, and descriptions of some of the highlights they will see. Maybe someone will sign up to go on the trip!

# Mrs. Frisby and the Rats of NIMH
## by Robert C. O'Brien

Chapter 20: The Main Hall
Chapter 21: The Toy Tinker
Chapter 22: Thorn Valley

Project 9: Art

The rats of NIMH had an unusual home under the rosebush. Re-create this unique home by using a large cardboard box to build a diorama of the inside of the main hall of the rats of NIMH. Include articles described in the book and any others you feel the rats would have had. Make a written comparison between those items found in the main hall and those the rats planned on having in Thorn Valley.

Consider these questions as you read these chapters: Were the rats going to live a simpler life without man's intervention? What was the main difference between the farm and Thorn Valley?

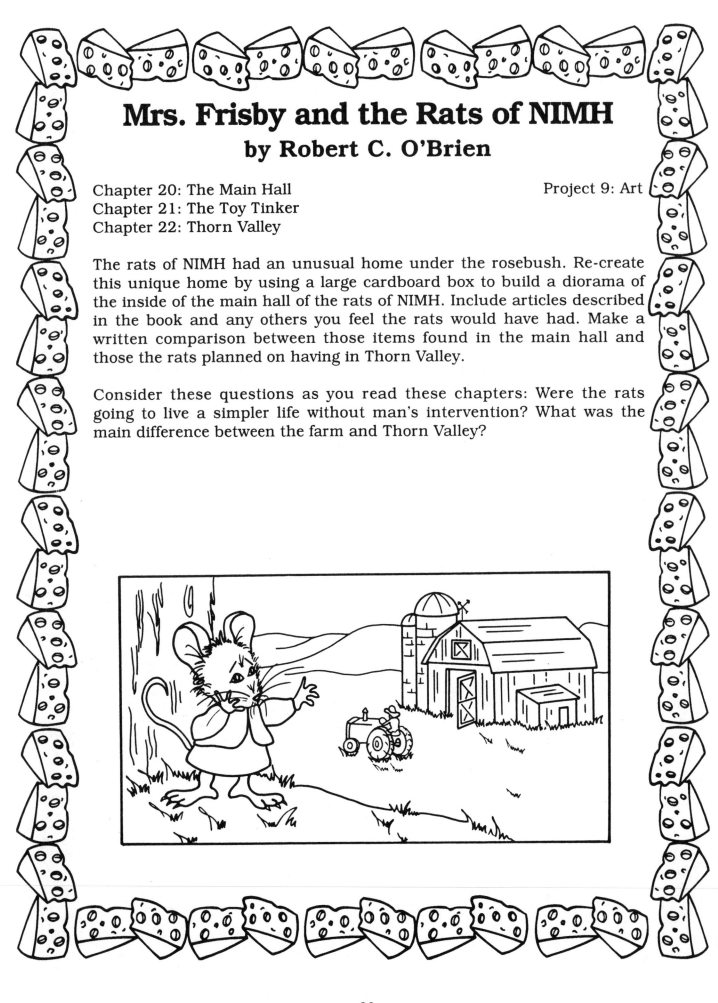

GA1425

# Mrs. Frisby and the Rats of NIMH
## by Robert C. O'Brien

Chapter 23: Captured
Chapter 24: Seven Dead Rats

Project 10: Physical Challenge

Play the Catch Mrs. Frisby playground game as follows:

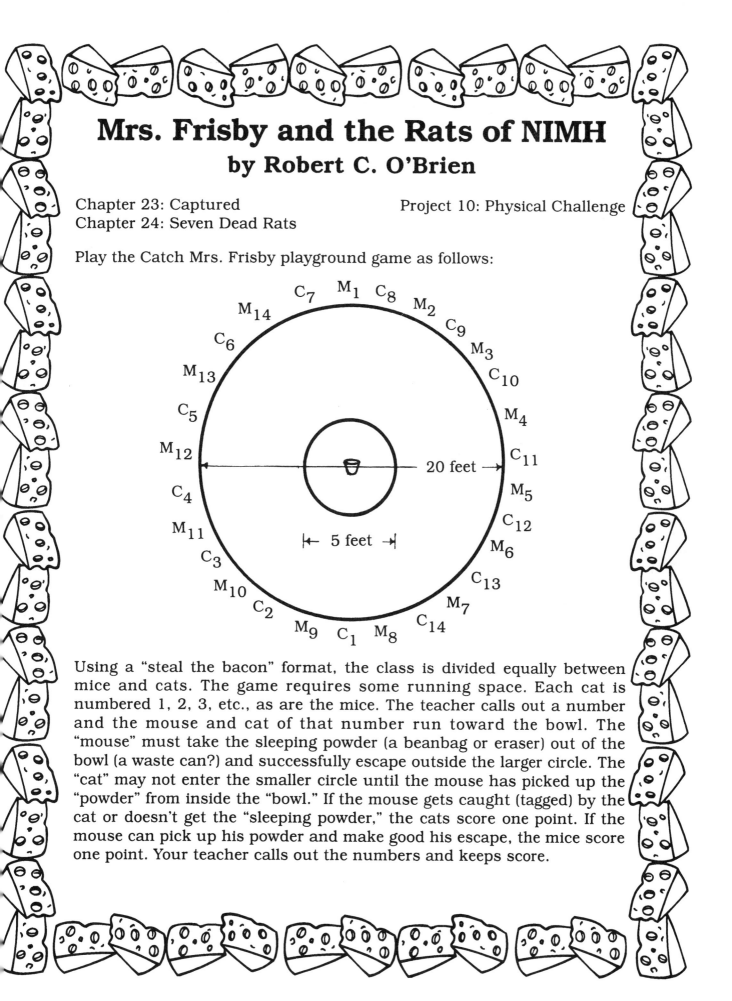

Using a "steal the bacon" format, the class is divided equally between mice and cats. The game requires some running space. Each cat is numbered 1, 2, 3, etc., as are the mice. The teacher calls out a number and the mouse and cat of that number run toward the bowl. The "mouse" must take the sleeping powder (a beanbag or eraser) out of the bowl (a waste can?) and successfully escape outside the larger circle. The "cat" may not enter the smaller circle until the mouse has picked up the "powder" from inside the "bowl." If the mouse gets caught (tagged) by the cat or doesn't get the "sleeping powder," the cats score one point. If the mouse can pick up his powder and make good his escape, the mice score one point. Your teacher calls out the numbers and keeps score.

GA1425

# Mrs. Frisby and the Rats of NIMH
## by Robert C. O'Brien

Chapter 25: Escape
Chapter 26: At the Meeting

Project 11: Writing

The rats were very helpful to Mrs. Frisby. Write a letter of thank you from Mrs. Frisby to the rats. Thank them for all their help; mention Mr. Frisby and wish them good luck in Thorn Valley.

GA1425

# Mrs. Frisby and the Rats of NIMH
## by Robert C. O'Brien

Chapter 27: The Doctor
Chapter 28: Epilogue

Project 12: Math

The rats had a formidable task of relocation ahead of them. Imagine you were going to start a colony in the wilderness. Each group member makes a list of all the necessary and desired items you would take. Keep the list realistic, manageable, and affordable. Estimate the cost of each item and find a total. From these separate lists make one list of items that everyone agrees on and, together with their costs, share your list with the class. See if your classmates agree with your list.

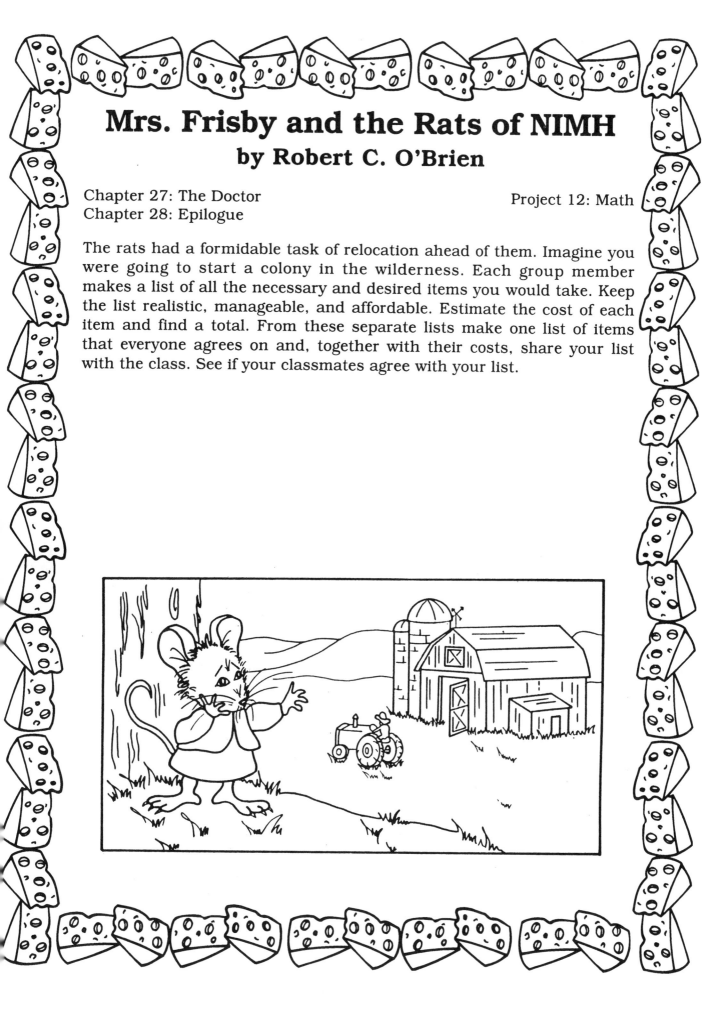

63

GA1425

# The Secret Garden
## by Frances Hodgson Burnett

Chapter 1: There's No One Left                    Project 1: Language
Chapter 2: Mistress Mary Quite Contrary

Mary Lennox spent the first years of her life in India with customs, traditions, and languages that may be different than yours. Pour through Chapters 1 and 2 to find the meaning of the words that follow. Make a language mobile that has the word and meaning plus an illustration that shows the meaning of the word. Also include a replica of India to dangle from the mobile. The words are *Ayah, Mem Sahib, Missie Sahib*.

# The Secret Garden
## by Frances Hodgson Burnett

Chapter 3: Across the Moor           Project 2: Social Studies
Chapter 4: Martha

The countryside and home at Misselthwaite Manor is quite different than Mary's home in India. By drawing or building three-dimensional objects, show the similarities and differences of the countryside and home in India and in England. Shoe boxes will work for the homes, construction and tissue paper will enhance the landscape along with the many other creative ideas of which your team will think.

GA1425

# The Secret Garden
## by Frances Hodgson Burnett

Chapter 5: A Cry in the Corridor

Chapter 6: "There Was Someone Crying–There Was"

Project 3: Reading

From deep inside the house Mary hears the cry of a human child. It continues on and on. The child must be soothed and your team has been chosen to do the job. Go back in your memories to the bedtime stories and lullabies and nursery rhymes that relax and help you fall asleep? Your team must pick five minutes of bedtime stories, nursery rhymes, etc., to read to the crying child (your class will stand in for the crying child). See if they relax and fall asleep!

GA1425

# The Secret Garden
## by Frances Hodgson Burnett

Chapter 7: The Key of the Garden

Project 4: Writing

Mary finds the key to the garden and will soon start a new experience. Imagine the key has special magical powers. Each person on your team will write a creative story about what the key can unlock for each of you. Read some of your stories to the class.

GA1425

# The Secret Garden
## by Frances Hodgson Burnett

Chapter: 8:  The Robin Who Showed the Way

Project 5: Physical Challenge

Martha brought Mary a present from across the moor. Mary's mother purchased the gift with money that was very scarce in her family. Find out what the gift is and "turn" this activity into a team game. This activity has been around for thousands of years. Until about one hundred years ago boys played this competitive game. As times changed girls took over the game and added rhymes. Make up some rhymes or use some you already know as your team gets into the swing of things. Since this is a competitive sport, get the rest of the teams involved in the game. Try this activity to the rhyme that is found in Chapter 2 about Mistress Mary.

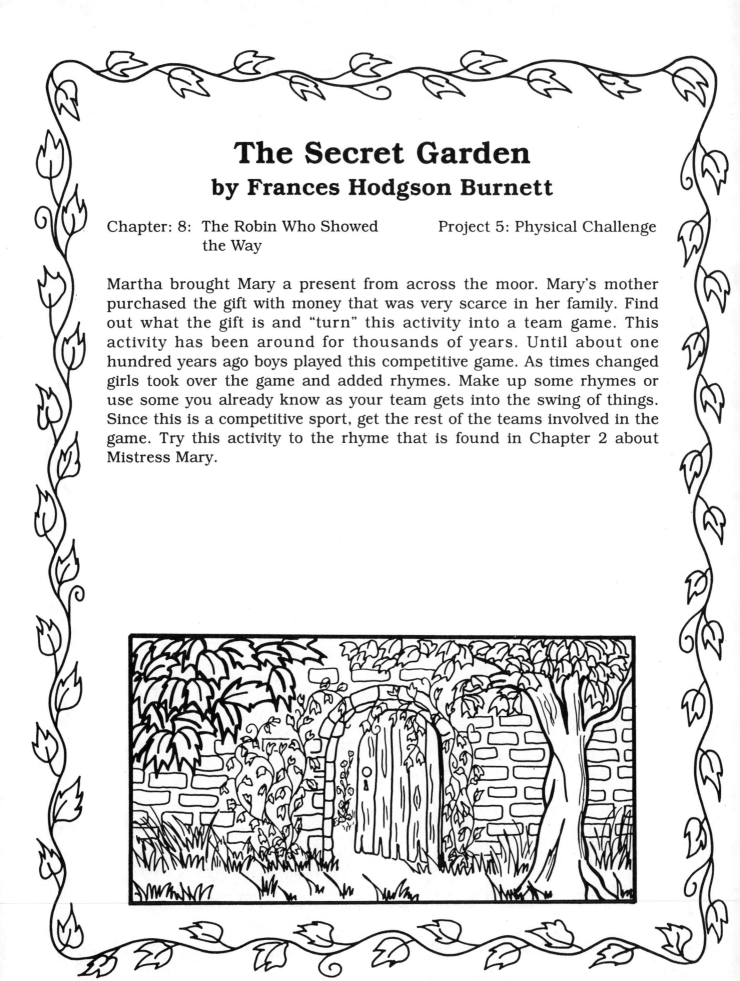

GA1425

# The Secret Garden
## by Frances Hodgson Burnett

Chapter 9: The Strangest House
Chapter 10: Dickon

Project 6: Art

Mary Lennox has found the joy of gardening, and it changes her life forever. A garden can be a beautiful picture anytime of the year. Mary finds the garden in early spring before many flowers are in bloom, but it did not stop her from envisioning what would soon follow in the garden. A French painter, Monet, devoted much of his painting career to painting gardens in watercolors. See if your team can find a picture of a watercolor painting that belongs to Monet. Next, have your team become Monets; and using watercolors, paint the Secret Garden, using some of Monet's techniques and colors. Turn a piece of the room into an art gallery and exhibit your paintings.

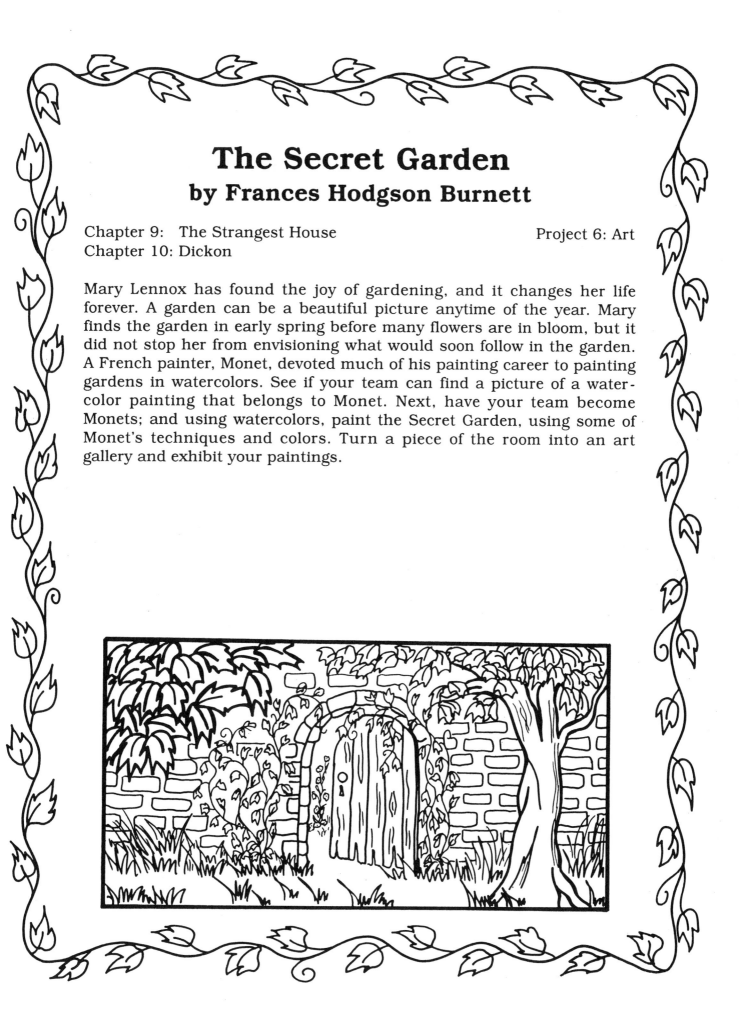

GA1425

# The Secret Garden
## by Frances Hodgson Burnett

Chapter 11: The Nest of the Missel Thrush
Chapter 12: "Might I Have a Bit of Earth?"
Chapter 13: "I Am Colin"
Chapter 14: A Young Rajeh
Chapter 15: Nest Building

Project 7: Math

Mary meets new people in these chapters. She meets drivers, cooks, maids, relatives, and more. Count how many people she meets starting when she steps off the train in England. Keep track of the people on the form below. You will have to go back a few chapters to get all the information.

## All Aboard

| Name of Person | Where Mary Met the Person | What Does the Person Do |
| --- | --- | --- |
|  |  |  |

GA1425

# The Secret Garden
## by Frances Hodgson Burnett

Chapter 16: "I Won't!" Said Mary

Project 8: Handwriting

As your team reads Chapter 16, you will see that a letter of thanks to Mr. Craven is necessary. Mary receives some wonderful items from Mr. Craven. Compose a letter to Mr. Craven thanking him for all the items that are in the packages. Even try to use the same writing tool that Mary received as a gift. Neat and tidy please! Post one copy on the bulletin board.

GA1425

# The Secret Garden
## by Frances Hodgson Burnett

Project 9: Drama

These chapters hold in store many fond memories for the reader plus a transition time in the characters' lives. Take the important information from these chapters and turn it into a readers' theater production. Practice and perform the readers' theater for the rest of the class.

GA1425

# The Secret Garden
## by Frances Hodgson Burnett

Chapter 23: Magic
Chapter 24: "Let Them Laugh"

Project 10: Cooking

Mary and Colin continue to eat and eat and to get healthier and healthier. It seems to the adults around them that they are eating more food than the adults are serving them, but that can't be. Little do the adults know! Plan a meal for Mary, Colin, Dickon, and your team outside among the fruits of the garden. Include some of the "extra things" that the children are eating, if possible. Mostly, have a leisurely picnic and enjoy the surroundings.

GA1425

# The Secret Garden
## by Frances Hodgson Burnett

Chapter 25: The Curtain                    Project 11: Science

The garden and the natural things around the Manor have come alive!
Brainstorm with your team members and make a list of flowers and
trees that come alive in the springtime. Draw a small sketch to go with
the things on your list. Post the sketches for your classmates to see.

GA1425

# The Secret Garden
## by Frances Hodgson Burnett

Chapter 26: "It's Mother!"
Chapter 27: In the Garden

Project 12: Music

Chapters 26 and 27 are the way all stories should end. Put the ending of this story to music and sing it to the class. Everyone knows the tune to "Mary Had a Little Lamb." Put your words to that tune and sing it up! You might want to videotape this production and show the tape to your class. Send a copy to your grandparents; they would be so proud.

GA1425

# The Cay
## by Theodore Taylor

Chapters 1-2                                                      Project 1: Art

Make a newspaper headline about the tragedy of the *S.S. Empire Tern*. Along with the headline, draw the scene of the *S.S. Empire Tern* as her tanks were being loaded. Include the sailors, onlookers and activities on board and off the ship. The second half of the scene must show what the ship looked like after she steamed out of St. Anna Bay and the torpedo hit. Add these before-and-after details that historians and news reporters tell and write about. Post the headline on the bulletin board.

                          GA1425

# The Cay
## by Theodore Taylor

Chapters 3-6                                Project 2: Drama

Reconstruct the raft scene by writing it as a play. Your play should include some of the following details: the people and cat on board, the vital provisions on the raft, the age of Timothy and Phillip and their health status, the dialects spoken, how long they spent on the raft, the dangers encountered on the raft, and any other details that your team feels necessary. Present your play to the class.

GA1425

# The Cay
## by Theodore Taylor

Chapter 7                                               Project 3: Social Studies

Curacao, one of the Netherlands Antilles Islands, is located in the Caribbean Sea off the coast of Venezuela. Using an atlas and sharing the work, make a map of the Caribbean Sea. As you read the story, use a dotted line to trace Phillip on his adventure. Place X's where major events occur. Go back to Chapter 3 for some latitude information if you need to. Post your map for your classmates to see.

GA1425

# The Cay
## by Theodore Taylor

Chapters 8-9                                    Project 4: Writing

After your team has read Chapters 8 and 9, discuss how the relationship between Phillip and Timothy has changed. Who has changed his opinion of the other person? How has being deserted with someone totally different from you affected each of you? How have prejudiced feelings changed? Will the two of them ever feel equal? Look at the dedication page at the beginning of the book. How does the dedication tie into these two chapters? After the team has discussed these questions, break up into two smaller groups. Have half of the team write down what they think would be Timothy's responses to the questions. The other half of the team writes down Phillip's responses to the questions. The paper can be written in diary or journal form. Compare one anothers' papers.

GA1425

# The Cay
## by Theodore Taylor

Chapter 10                                              Project 5: Cooking

The diet of Timothy and Phillip changed drastically while they were on the island. One of their staples turned out to be coconuts. Bring some coconuts into class and share the milk and meat with your classmates. If your coconut trees are bare, bring in shredded coconut or coconut macaroons.

GA1425

# The Cay
## by Theodore Taylor

Chapter 11

Project 6: Reading

There are many spiritual and religious beliefs around the world. You read of one belief in Chapter 11. Do some research on religions and pick five to illustrate on a mobile. Hang the mobile in your classroom.

# The Cay
## by Theodore Taylor

Chapter 12                                      Project 7: Science

One of the characters is suffering from malaria. Phillip does not know what to do for Timothy! Your "medical" team's mission is to beam to the island to diagnose this disease, give it a name, and explain its symptoms, how to treat the disease, and the prognosis for recovery. For your medical trip, take (make) some pictures of the malaria cycle and how the mosquito helps transmit the disease. Share your information with Phillip. Your classmates will represent Phillip (short trip, huh) so be prepared to give your medical presentation to the class.

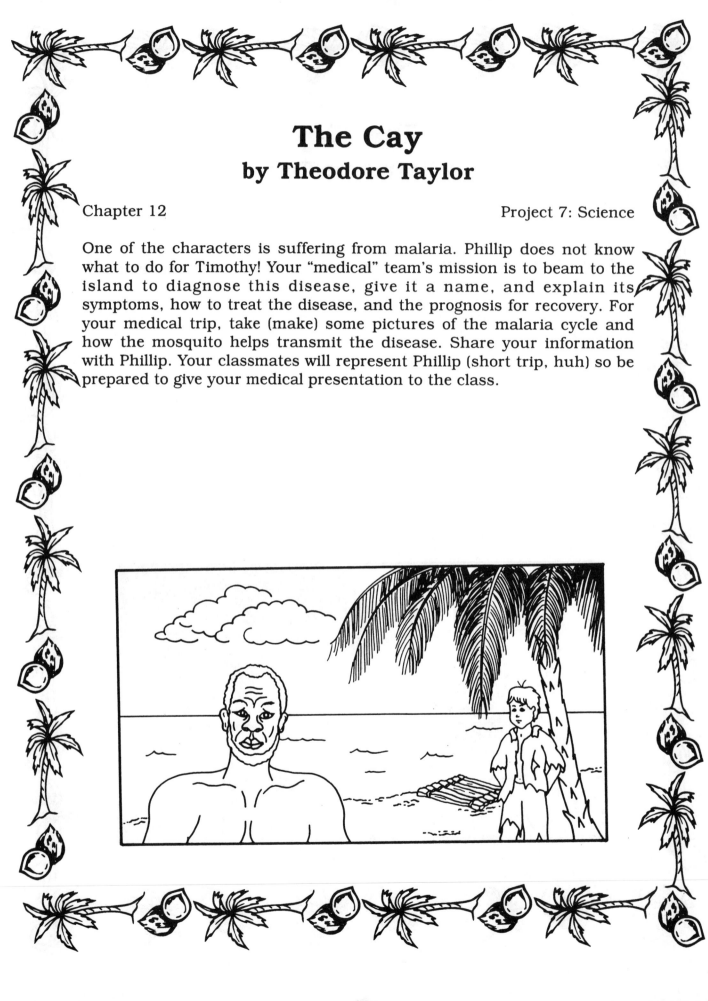

GA1425

# The Cay
## by Theodore Taylor

Chapter 13                                              Project 8: Math

Phillip devised a way to keep track of the days while they were stranded on the cay. He also knew the approximate time of day. How could a blind person devise such tools?

Your team's challenge is to come up with a couple of ways to tell time and days passed. You may not use the same devices that Phillip used. To make things more challenging, pretend that you are blind. Design and build the devices so they tell/show/feel that you have been stranded for seventy-three days. Explain to the class how your time telling and calendar devices work.

# The Cay
## by Theodore Taylor

Chapter 14                                        Project 9: Language

Identify Timothy's dialect. Practice talking with the same dialect. The paragraph in which Timothy describes the Hettie Redd mishap is a good one to practice. After your team feels comfortable with the dialect, formulate a new paragraph that would fit Timothy's personality and experience. Incorporate some of Timothy's music that he sings while on the cay.

When you have the paragraph and music perfect, "recite" it to the class. See if your audience can interpret your paragraph and song.

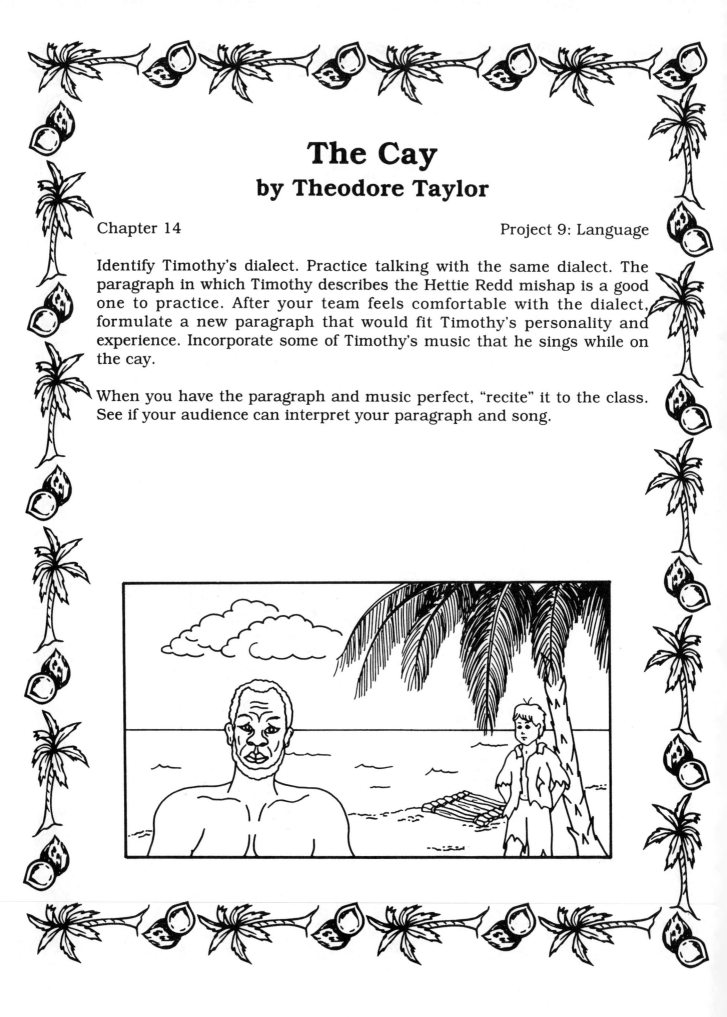

GA1425

# The Cay
## by Theodore Taylor

Chapter 15                                    Project 10: Handwriting

After you read this painful chapter, try to think of yourself in such a predicament! Each member of your group must write Phillip's pleas for help; do it blindfolded.

Put the messages in a bottle and present them to other classmates. See if they can decipher the messages.

85

GA1425

# The Cay
## by Theodore Taylor

Chapters 16-17                    Project 11: Physical Challenge

The cay was littered with debris, and as you read these chapters you will find out it was somewhat dangerous for Phillip. His fishing expedition is not what you call safe either. Imagine being in the middle of such a mess! Instead of imagining the mess, simulate the messy cay. Devise an obstacle cay using at least ten of the items that were washed ashore. Here's the "catch"; your victims (classmates) must go through the obstacle course blindfolded to simulate Phillip's disability.

When they start through the course, they start with twenty points. Every time they step on debris subtract a point. Change the course slightly for every victim and keep track of their points. Give the winners "tacky prizes."

GA1425

# The Cay
## by Theodore Taylor

Chapters 17-18

Project 12: Music

With all the sounds that are described in these chapters, compile an audiotape that simulates some of the sounds. See how many of the sounds your team can duplicate.

Have the class listen to the tape and see who can correctly identify the most sounds.

GA1425

# Where the Red Fern Grows
## by Wilson Rawls

Chapters 1-3                                    Project 1: Drama

The opening chapters set the stage for a wonderful remembrance of a boy's childhood. With the help of everyone on your team, turn Chapters 1-3 into a readers' theater.

Billy, as an adult, will easily become the narrator that drifts back to the days when the painful yearning for hound dogs becomes reality. Have everyone on your team be involved in writing and/or acting out the readers' theater. Present your play to your classmates.

GA1425

# Where the Red Fern Grows
## by Wilson Rawls

Chapters 4-5             Project 2: Social Studies

Billy took a long, tough journey to get his pups at the railway station. Turn his journey into a board game using some of Billy's experiences on his journey to add challenge to the game. Incorporate the geography in the Oklahoma hills and the small town layout to add authenticity to the game.

After you have made the board, graphics, rules, etc., play the game to see if you have a marketable product. Other class members may want to play your game.

GA1425

# Where the Red Fern Grows
## by Wilson Rawls

Chapters 6-7                                                    Project 3: Reading

Skim Chapters 1, 2, and 3 of the book *Rascal* by Sterling North. The raccoon in *Rascal* is presented in a different light than the raccoons in *Where the Red Fern Grows*. Compare and contrast the differences in the treatment of raccoons in these two books.

Put your comparisons together in the form of a mobile that you will hang in the classroom.

# Where the Red Fern Grows
## by Wilson Rawls

Chapters 8-9                                                    Project 4: Art

Make a diorama of the scenes in Chapters 8 and 9 with Billy and the big sycamore tree. It should include the beginning scene found in Chapter 8 and the final scene found in Chapter 9. You may find paper towel rolls to be helpful in replicating the tree.

Share your finished product with your class.

GA1425

# Where the Red Fern Grows
## by Wilson Rawls

Chapters 10-11                                                    Project 5: Music

Write lyrics to tell about the "goings on" in these two chapters. Set the lyrics to a familiar tune. Chapter 10 should be verse one and Chapter 11 should be verse two. Include a refrain easy enough for everyone in your class to learn quickly.

Sing the song to the class.

                                       GA1425

# Where the Red Fern Grows
## by Wilson Rawls

Chapters 12-13                    Project 6: Writing

Write an article that could have appeared in the local community newspaper regarding the tragedy in the mountains. Give background information about the boys and their dogs and other events that led up to the accident.

Post the article in the room.

                    GA1425

# Where the Red Fern Grows
## by Wilson Rawls

Chapter 14                                    Project 7: Handwriting

Billy's grandfather introduces Billy to the biggest adventure he could have imagined, a coon hunt contest. Grandfather took care of the record keeping and the letters and the entry fee, and he probably even received a letter of acceptance to tell him that Old Dan and Little Ann qualified for the hunt.

It is your team's challenge to duplicate one of the requirements of Grandpa's record keeping. Each team member must write a letter that says why Grandpa thought Billy and his dogs were qualified to be in the hunting contest. Write with a pen in your neatest handwriting. Choose the most qualified letter to read to the class.

GA1425

# Where the Red Fern Grows
## by Wilson Rawls

Chapter 15                                              Project 8: Math

The dogs that attended the big hunt were chosen as the best from miles around. Although the book just lists the success of the finalists, the woods must have been filled with raccoons. Suppose the twenty-five pairs of dogs were divided evenly to hunt the five days. If the contestants who didn't qualify for the runoff averaged one raccoon per pair of dogs, based on the information provided in the book, how many raccoons were taken during the hunt, including the championship?

GA1425

# Where the Red Fern Grows
## by Wilson Rawls

Chapters 16-17                                        Project 9: Cooking

The good down-home taste of homemade ice cream is always the best. Your team can make homemade ice cream to share with the rest of the class. This is what you'll need:

  3 large clean coffee cans
  3 small clean coffee cans that will fit inside the large cans
  duct tape
  ice
  rock salt
  spoons and paper cups

In a big bowl mix

| | |
|---|---|
| 1 big can condensed milk | 1 box vanilla pudding |
| 5 eggs | pinch of salt |
| 2 cups (480 ml) sugar | 2 T. (30 ml) vanilla |
| regular milk to fill each small can three-fourths full | |

Divide and pour the ice cream recipe into the three small coffee cans and tightly tape their lids shut. Each can should be about three-fourths full. Place the cans inside the large cans. Add ice and lots of rock salt between the small and large cans. Tightly tape the lid on the large can. Roll the cans back and forth to a partner for about twenty-five minutes. The ice cream should be cold and delicious! Share with all. If you need more ice cream, double the recipe.

GA1425

# Where the Red Fern Grows
## by Wilson Rawls

Chapter 18                                                    Project 10: Science

Grandpa has an accident in this part of the book and ends up with a very nasty sprained ankle. It is bad enough that he has to have a cast on his ankle. Make a replica of Grandpa's cast out of plaster of Paris. After the plaster dries, do what everyone does to a cast. Write all the team members' names on it!

GA1425

# Where the Red Fern Grows
## by Wilson Rawls

Chapter 19                    Project 11: Physical Challenge

The fight with the mountain lion must have felt like it lasted forever, but in truth it was probably less than three minutes. Three minutes of physical exertion of that caliber is totally exhausting.

Your team must think of some sort of physical game that lasts three minutes that can be played in the confines of your classroom. A timer could be used to keep track of the time frame. It must be a team game that all can participate in, and it must be totally exhausting (tug-of-war).

GA1425

# Where the Red Fern Grows
## by Wilson Rawls

Chapter 20                                    Project 12: Language

Construct a book cover for *Where the Red Fern Grows*. The cover should include a drawing and a short description of the book and author. "Sell" this book to the rest of the class with the book cover, and then display it on the bulletin board for all to see.

GA1425

# From the Mixed-Up Files of Mrs. Basil E. Frankweiler
## by E.L. Konigsburg

Chapter 1                                    Project 1: Physical Challenge

On the bus to school, the four Kincaid children, Claudia, Jamie, Kevin, and Steve, sit two to a seat. How many possible seating arrangements are there for the four children? How many possible arrangements would there be if Jamie and Kevin always sit next to a window? Using paper, calculate your answers. Act out the possible arrangements to check your solutions.

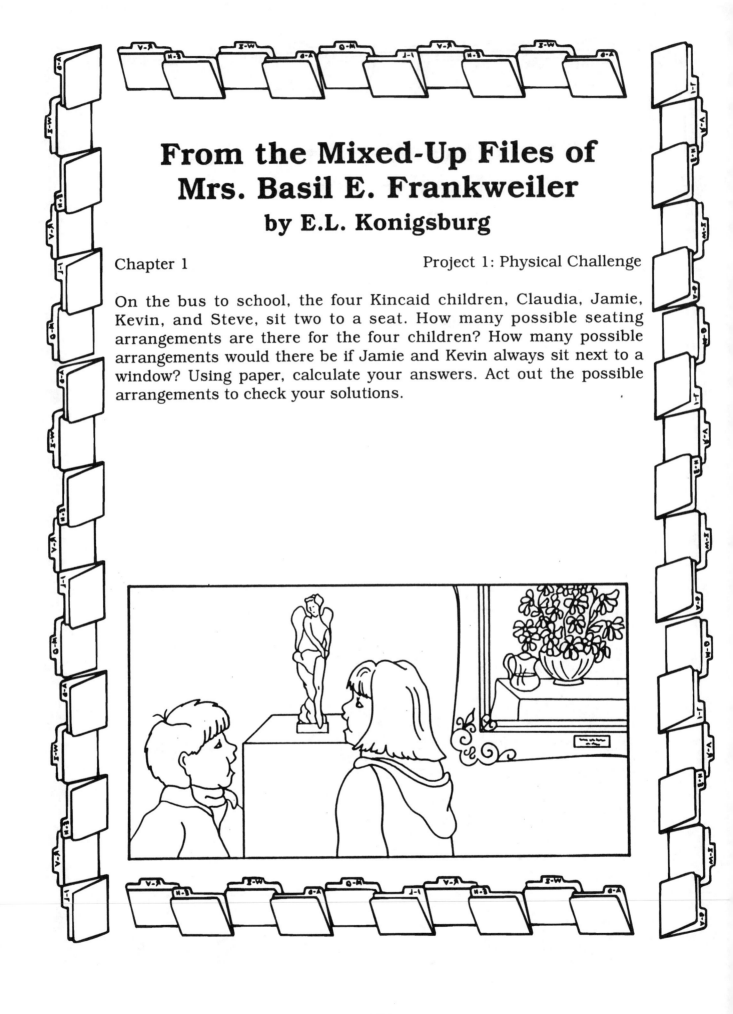

GA1425

# From the Mixed-Up Files of Mrs. Basil E. Frankweiler
## by E.L. Konigsburg

Chapter 1                                    Project 2: Math

Claudia thought Jamie might end up as a business tycoon someday because he had accumulated $24.43. Pretend your group has undertaken an adventure like Jamie's and Claudia's. Design a budget that will feed all members of your group for one week. Take into account that you cannot cook any foods but must either purchase prepared foods or select foods that do not need cooking. Make a chart to show your daily menu and its cost. Post your menu for your classmates to see.

GA1425

# From the Mixed-Up Files of Mrs. Basil E. Frankweiler

## by E.L. Konigsburg

Chapter 2                                      Project 3: Social Studies

Jamie wants to hide out in New York City's Central Park, 840 acres of grass, trees and rolling hills. Known as the "Big Apple," New York City has many famous sights. From Broadway and Times Square to the Statue of Liberty and Coney Island, New York City is loaded with sights to delight tourists visiting this largest city on the eastern seaboard. Research and make a list of at least ten of the most famous sights of New York City that your group would like to see. Post your list and see how it compares with the choices of your classmates.

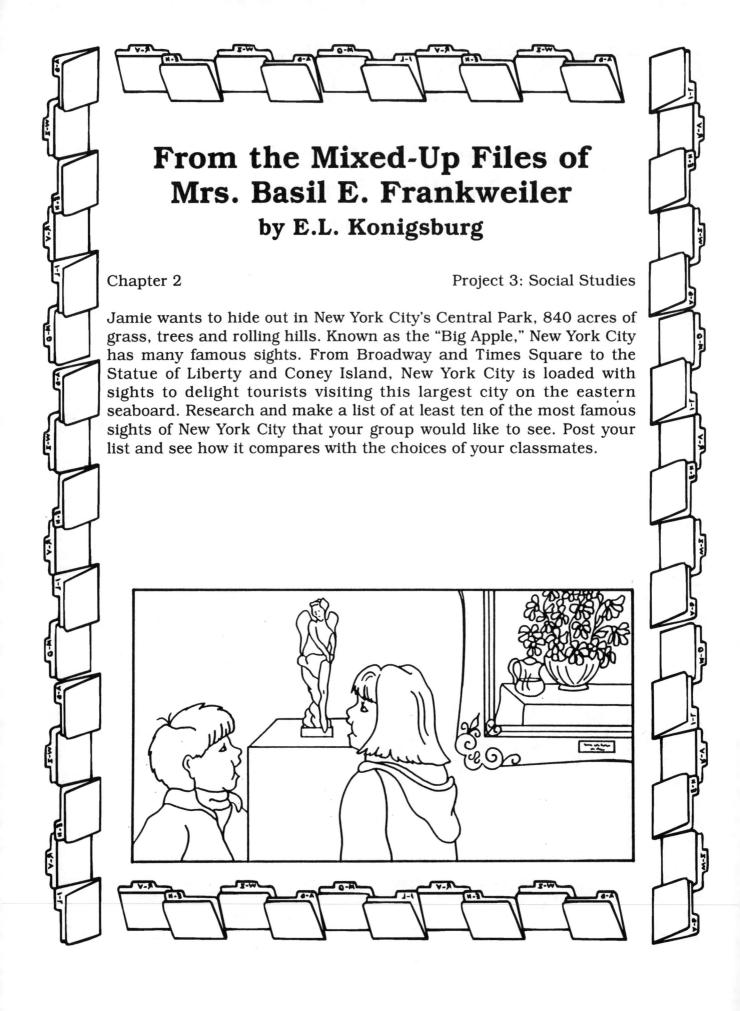

GA1425

# From the Mixed-Up Files of Mrs. Basil E. Frankweiler
## by E.L. Konigsburg

Chapter 3                                          Project 4: Science

In Chapter 3, Jamie uses a compass to find his directions. Using a compass, have each member of your team set up an orienteering course and challenge the other members of your class to follow it. An example for the beginning of a possible orienteering course might be:

"From the classroom door, head due north 10 steps; head southwest 3 steps and due east 5 steps."

As you develop your orienteering course you may wish to make it more difficult by using the numerical degrees on your compass. Plot your directions on a card, buy or tape a small treasure (a penny or a gum ball?) at the end of the orienteering course and have fun challenging your teammates to find your treasure. This course could be set up inside the room or, with the teacher's permission, outside or on the playground. Enjoy your treasure hunt!

GA1425

# From the Mixed-Up Files of Mrs. Basil E. Frankweiler
## by E.L. Konigsburg

Chapter 4                                                      Project 5: Writing

Write an article for the newspaper about the missing kids. Be sure to include descriptions, both physical and psychological, and as many facts as possible. You may wish to make your "missing person report" like those found on the side of milk cartons. Whichever way you choose, post this "missing person report" for the class to see.

                                                      GA1425

# From the Mixed-Up Files of Mrs. Basil E. Frankweiler
## by E.L. Konigsburg

Chapter 5                                                    Project 6: Art

Michelangelo Buonarroti was born in 1475 and went on to become a leader in the Renaissance (rebirth of culture and learning) and became one of the most famous artists in history.

Research the works of Michelangelo and make a clay or papier-mâché statue of "Angel," as you believe it might have looked. After completing the statue, cover the statue with a coating of plaster of Paris and spray it with clear fixative or clear enamel to give it a marble "sheen." This may take a few days to complete. Display your finished product for the class to see.

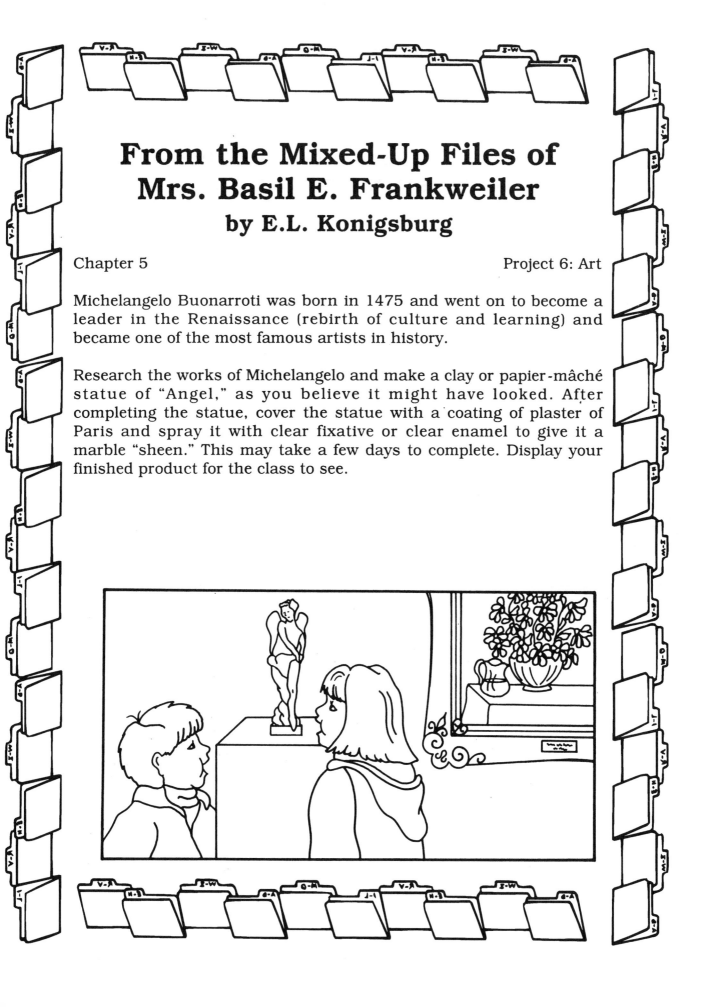

GA1425

# From the Mixed-Up Files of Mrs. Basil E. Frankweiler
## by E.L. Konigsburg

Chapter 6                              Project 7: Handwriting

Claudia was worried that her handwriting needed to be disguised when they sent their letter to the museum. Have each member of your class make a copy of the letter using different methods of disguise. Some suggestions are

  cut the words/letters from newspapers
  write in calligraphy
  write in a foreign language
  use a picture (or pictures) to tell the message

Display your letters for the class to see.

GA1425

# From the Mixed-Up Files of Mrs. Basil E. Frankweiler
## by E.L. Konigsburg

Chapter 7                    Project 8: Language

Secrets can be fun, and journeys can be as well. A secret journey can have a double pleasure.

Claudia and Jamie have started to enjoy their secret journey. Using vocabulary words from the book, write a poem about the Metropolitan Museum of Art. Work as a group, illustrate your poem, and post it where it can be seen by your classmates.

107

# From the Mixed-Up Files of Mrs. Basil E. Frankweiler
## by E.L. Konigsburg

Chapter 8                                              Project 9: Drama

Claudia wants to come back "different" from her adventure than when she left. An easy way to be different is by using a disguise. Every member of your team should wear a disguise to school tomorrow and be ready to explain how the disguise makes him feel different. Share this feeling of difference with your class in a short presentation.

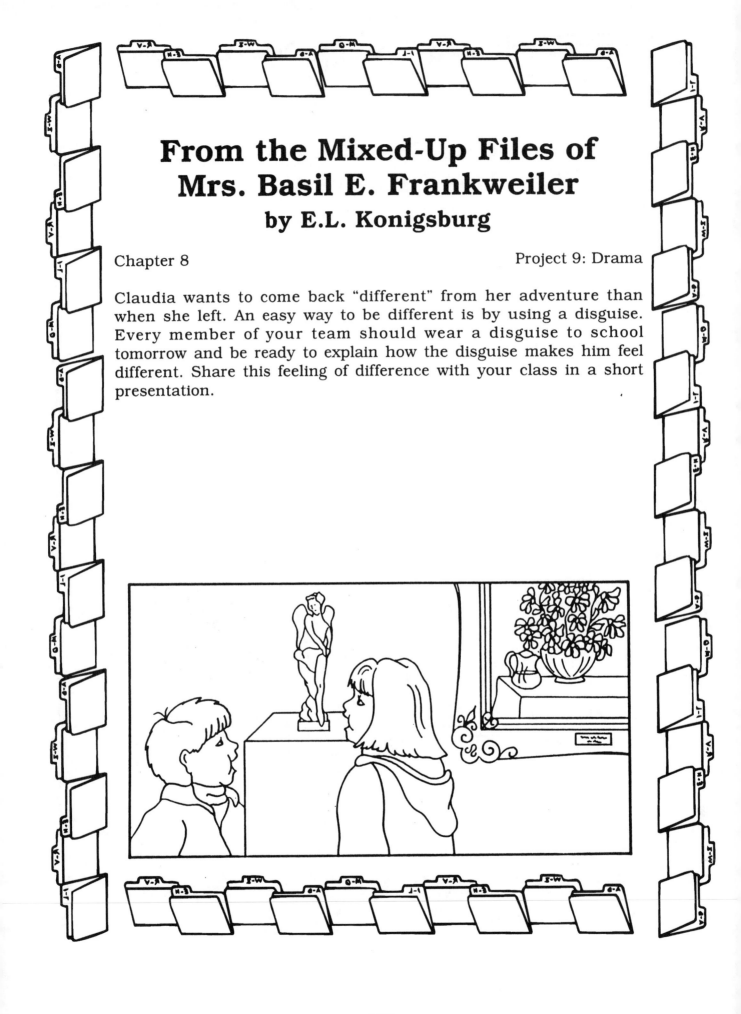

GA1425

# From the Mixed-Up Files of Mrs. Basil E. Frankweiler
## by E.L. Konigsburg

Chapter 9                                    Project 10: Reading

In many books, characters, especially children, grow and change in the story to end up "different" from what they were at the beginning of the story. Think about other books you have read and list how the main characters change. Examples of books you might choose are

*Where the Red Fern Grows* by Wilson Rawls
*Call It Courage* by Armstrong Sperry
*The Cay* by Theodore Taylor
*The Westing Game* by Ellen Raskin
*The Indian in the Cupboard* by Lynne Reid Banks

As a team, make a list of books whose characters undergo changes, list those changes, and post the list for the class to see.

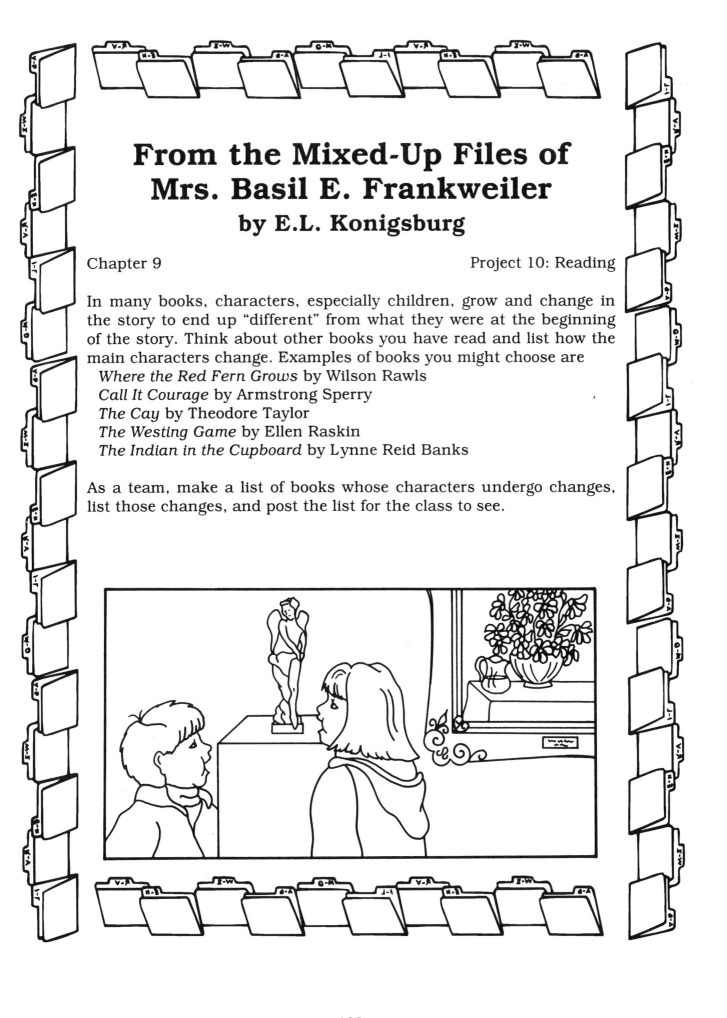

GA1425

# From the Mixed-Up Files of Mrs. Basil E. Frankweiler
## by E.L. Konigsburg

Chapter 9                                    Project 11: Cooking

Jamie and Claudia enjoyed the "Novilles et fromage en casserole" that Mrs. Basil E. Frankweiler served them for lunch. It turned out to be a rather ordinary lunch under all the fancy trappings. Your job is to create one snack per team member to share with your class tomorrow. The snack may be of your choice; however, before you serve it you must give it a fancy name. After hearing what you intend to share with them, let your classmates guess what it will be. Perhaps you'll give it a French, German, Italian, or Spanish name. Whatever you choose, play the role of a great chef.

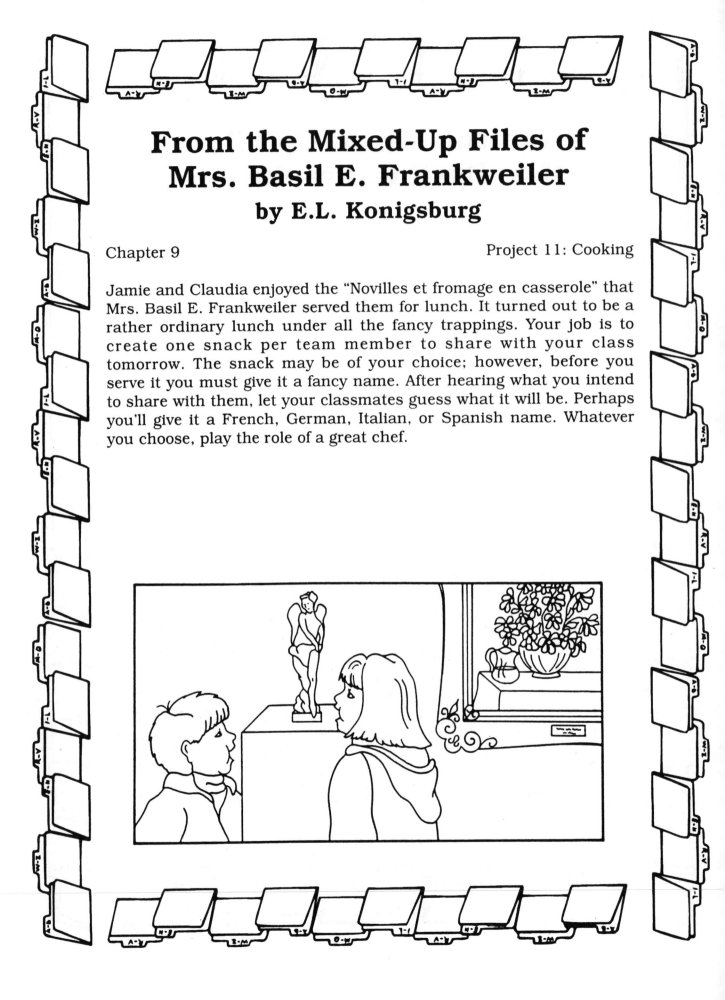

GA1425

# From the Mixed-Up Files of Mrs. Basil E. Frankweiler
## by E.L. Konigsburg

Chapter 10                                               Project 12: Music

Many times music has the ability to add insight to a story. Make up your own song about Jamie's and Claudia's adventure.

Choose a popular melody (a slow one is best) with which everyone on your team is familiar. Change the words so it tells the story of Jamie and Claudia. Such a ballad is a good musical way to tell a story. Have each member of your team take one or two chapters and write the words to tell what happened in that section of the book. As a group, sing this finished song for the class.

          GA1425

# A Wrinkle in Time
## by Madeleine L'Engle

Chapter 1: Mrs. Whatsit                                    Project 1: Art

Re-create the kitchen scene on this dark and stormy night. Include all the characters that eventually end up in the kitchen. Add any other rooms of the house that are mentioned in the reading of Chapter 1. Make this project three dimensional by using a cardboard box, shoe box, etc.

GA1425

# A Wrinkle in Time
## by Madeleine L'Engle

Chapter 2: Mrs. Who                    Project 2: Drama

Chapter 2 lends itself to a great readers' theater. There are lots of characters and emotions running through this chapter. This chapter sets the stage for Meg's self-esteem doubts and problems at school. Your team must write and act out the play. Make sure your actors portray the suspense that is lurking in this part of the book. Perform the play for your class.

GA1425

# A Wrinkle in Time
## by Madeleine L'Engle

Chapter 1: Mrs. Whatsit
Chapter 2: Mrs. Who
Chapter 3: Mrs. Which

Project 3: Language

These three ladies are quite the characters! It is questionable if any like them exist elsewhere. Turn the characters into a three-page "pop-up" book for students, describing each one with exciting language that will stimulate others to read the book. When finished, share the book with the class.

GA1425

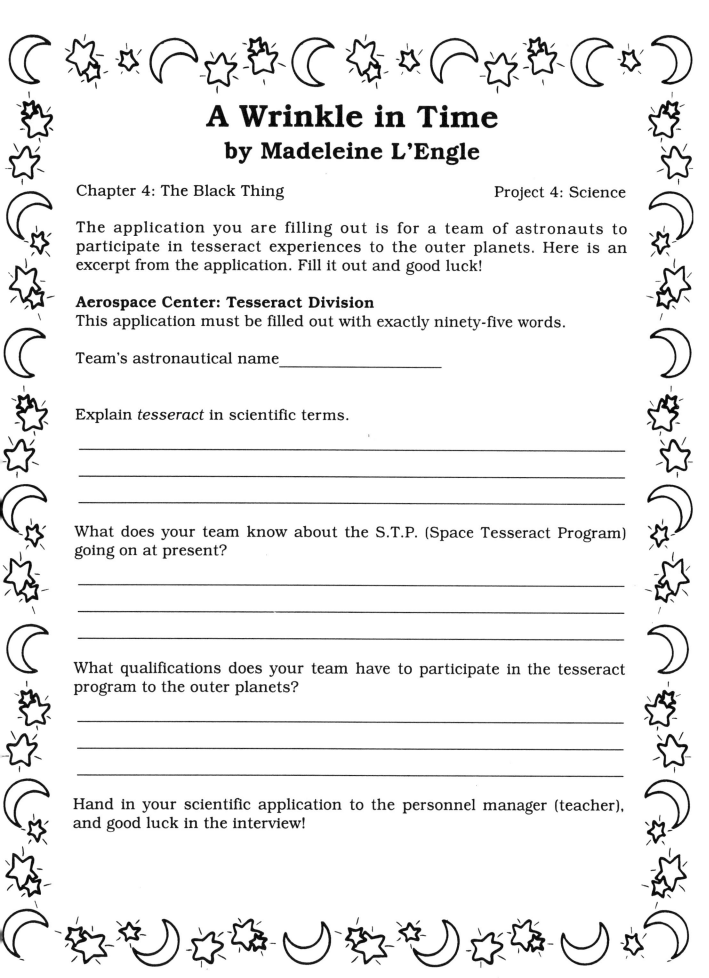

# A Wrinkle in Time
## by Madeleine L'Engle

Chapter 4: The Black Thing                    Project 4: Science

The application you are filling out is for a team of astronauts to participate in tesseract experiences to the outer planets. Here is an excerpt from the application. Fill it out and good luck!

**Aerospace Center: Tesseract Division**
This application must be filled out with exactly ninety-five words.

Team's astronautical name_____

Explain *tesseract* in scientific terms.

_____
_____
_____

What does your team know about the S.T.P. (Space Tesseract Program) going on at present?

_____
_____
_____

What qualifications does your team have to participate in the tesseract program to the outer planets?

_____
_____
_____

Hand in your scientific application to the personnel manager (teacher), and good luck in the interview!

                                       GA1425

# A Wrinkle in Time
## by Madeleine L'Engle

Chapter 5: The Tesseract                    Project 5: Cooking

As Meg, Calvin and Charles Wallace journey on, they are reminded that they are hungry. With the help from the crystal ball, put together a restaurant menu from the planet where your team thinks they may be in this chapter. Make the menu appealing, colorful and descriptive. Be sure the menu comes from an acceptable restaurant from those parts. Include prices and the kind of money accepted and, of course, children's portions. Provide a few food samples for the class.

# A Wrinkle in Time
## by Madeleine L'Engle

Chapter 6: The Happy Medium                    Project 6: Physical Challenge

The advice from one of the guardians to the children is good advice for your team for this activity. The challenge is to find a partner on your team, stand back-to-back and lock arms. Both of you lower your bodies to the ground and try to get back up without separating. See how many times you can go down and get back up in one minute. Your teacher will want to see this activity for sure! You may even want to challenge another team. Remember the advice; do not let them separate you!

GA1425

# A Wrinkle in Time
## by Madeleine L'Engle

Chapter 7: The Man with Red Eyes                    Project 7: Writing

The properties of persuasion are very powerful as you have read in Chapter 7. Your team has just been granted the privilege to tamper with the balance in the classroom through a persuasion activity. You will take over the role as the Man with the Red Eyes. Decide what the neatest activity is in this class.

Now, your team must write a paper addressed to the entire class and the teacher, stating why you think the best thing that ever happened to this class must be stopped. Your argument must be convincing and the class should think that you are dead serious. Your teacher will give you time to present this activity. Let your teacher know that he/she should go along with the elimination of the neatest thing in the classroom. After your team has won over the hearts and minds of the entire class (it had better be a good persuasion), you may disclose that it was only an activity to show how a convincing leader (your team) can overpower even the best things in your life.

GA1425

# A Wrinkle in Time
## by Madeleine L'Engle

Chapter 8: The Transparent Column                    Project 8: Math

The building that the children are in is quite unique with the special walls, elevators, etc. How would you like your school to look like the transparent building? It will cost your school $100.00 per square foot to rebuild and look like the building described in Chapter 8. Estimate the cost of a new school with the same square footage that it has now. Submit your estimate to your teacher.

GA1425

# A Wrinkle in Time
## by Madeleine L'Engle

Chapter 9: It                                          Project 9: Music

As you read through Chapter 9, the subjects of concentration, rhythm, and rhymes are key components. It seems that it is good to have rhythm in this place. Your team's challenge is to write a musical rhyme to the tune of "Mary Had a Little Lamb" about this chapter. After you have composed the words, sing the song to the class. The song must be produced with the zombie-like monotones that are found in this chapter. Pretend as though you were under It's command. Include a verse in your song that tells about what the children and their father do on the last page of this chapter.

GA1425

# A Wrinkle in Time
## by Madeleine L'Engle

Chapter 10: Absolute Zero
Chapter 11: Aunt Beast

Project 10: Social Studies

There are references to the solar system, Earth and other planets in these chapters that may give your team some ideas as to where the "travelers" are. With your spacial, astronomical and geographical skills, design a map of our solar system to include some of the new places discovered in *A Wrinkle in Time*. Incorporate what we know to be true of the planets and solar system with the new information in the book. You will position the new places somewhere between fact and fantasy to unveil new answers to our solar system. Post the adjusted solar system in your classroom.

GA1425

# A Wrinkle in Time
## by Madeleine L'Engle

Chapter 11: Aunt Beast                    Project 11: Handwriting

Devise a written language for the Beasts that we meet in this chapter. They have different appendages, so take that into account when your team invents the written language. They may use a new form of our alphabet, or their written language may be with pictures or maybe with brand-new symbols.

Rewrite the paragraph in Chapter 11 that starts like this..."Aunt Beast lifted Meg onto the bench and sat down beside her." Of course the rewrite should be in the Beast's written language that you have invented. Post the new language and see if your classmates can decipher it.

GA1425

# A Wrinkle in Time
## by Madeleine L'Engle

Chapter 12: The Foolish and the Weak

Project 12: Reading

The climax is at hand. After reading this final chapter, ask each other if there are other books that you have read that have similar endings. Your team may come up with quite a few. Choose two of the similar books and read the ending passages out loud to your teacher. Be ready to explain why you chose the books you chose as having the same sort of ending as *A Wrinkle in Time*.

GA1425

# Danny,
# the Champion of the World
## by Roald Dahl

Chapter 1: The Filling Station
Chapter 2: The Big Friendly Giant

Project 1: Art

The wonderful gypsy caravan that Danny and his dad called home was over a hundred and fifty years old. Research gypsies and their caravans. Reread the section of the book describing the caravan and, using this knowledge and the pictures in the book, make a cardboard copy of the caravan. Make your caravan a "cutaway" on one side to show the inside. When presenting your model to the class, give a short report on the history of caravans and gypsies.

GA1425

# Danny,
# the Champion of the World
## by Roald Dahl

Chapter 3: Cars and Kits and Fire Balloons                    Project 2: Science

Danny's father seemed to be a great dad because of the fun ideas he had. You're going to build a kite that will really fly. Follow the directions below to make a miniature bow kite.

**Materials:**
two 6" (15.24 cm) broom straws or plastic drinking straws
7" x 7" (17.78 x 17.78 cm) square piece of tissue paper (or thin plastic bag)
heavy sewing thread
glue

**Instructions:**
Lay the cross (bow) straw 2" (5.08 cm) from the top of the spine straw and fasten them together securely using several wraps of thread (Figure 1). String together the tips of all four points of the two straws using thread (Figure 2). Run a crossing thread from tip to tip causing the bow straw to "bow" slightly. Lay the framework on the tissue paper and cut around it allowing 1" (2.54 cm) all the way around. Fold this extra inch over the string and glue it. Put a drop of glue at tips of straws where thread is and where straws cross. Allow to dry (Figure 3).

The next steps are very important. Your bridle thread must be placed in the correct position or your kite will have trouble flying.

Make two small holes in the paper, midway from the crossing point to the top of the spine and midway from the bottom of the spine to the crossing point (Figure 4). Carefully run a thread through the hole and firmly tie it to the spine in both places. Allow about 2" (5.08 cm) of slack in this bridle. Tie your sewing thread to this bridle as shown. Some slight adjustments may be necessary and a tissue paper tail can be added. Now...GO FLY A KITE!

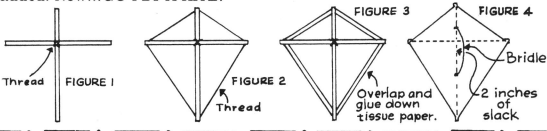

FIGURE 3    FIGURE 4

Thread | FIGURE I

FIGURE 2
Thread

Overlap and glue down tissue paper.

Bridle

2 inches of slack

GA1425

# Danny,
# the Champion of the World
## by Roald Dahl

Chapter 4: My Father's Deep Dark Secret          Project 3: Language
Chapter 5: The Secret Methods

Danny's father states his own dad was a splendiferous poacher. The word *splendiferous* is a made-up word (called a portmanteau). If you were to take two words such as *grand* and *fantastic*, you could create a new word *grandtastic*. Create several such new words yourself and post your list of new compound words (complete with definitions) where the class can see them.

GA1425

# Danny, the Champion of the World
## by Roald Dahl

Chapter 6: Mr. Victor Hazell                    Project 4: Math
Chapter 7: The Baby Austin

While traveling in the Baby Austin, Danny made some calculations about speed, distance, and time. He knew that travelling at a speed of 60 miles per hour you travel one mile in one minute.

Work as a group to complete this chart. Show your teacher when you are finished.

| 60 mph | = | 1 mile   | in | 1 minute   |
|--------|---|----------|----|------------|
| 60 mph | = | 2 miles  | in | ___ minutes |
| 30 mph | = | 1 mile   | in | ___ minutes |
| 10 mph | = | 10 miles | in | ___ minutes |
| 60 mph | = | ___ miles | in | 20 minutes |
| 30 mph | = | ___ miles | in | 30 minutes |
| ___ mph | = | 20 miles | in | 40 minutes |
| ___ mph | = | 30 miles | in | 30 minutes |

The space shuttle can travel around the earth (about 25,000 miles) in one hour. Its speed, then, is 25,000 miles per hour.

A snail can travel about one mile in approximately 30 hours. Its speed would be about .03 mph.

After taking your own guess, use an almanac to obtain the rates of speed for these creatures.

| Animal  | Guess | Actual |
|---------|-------|--------|
| Cheetah |       |        |
| Lion    |       |        |
| Coyote  |       |        |
| Rabbit  |       |        |

GA1425

# Danny,
# the Champion of the World
## by Roald Dahl

Chapter 8: The Pit
Chapter 9: Doc Spencer

Project 5: Writing

Danny showed skill, bravery, and daring when he rescued his father from the pit in Hazell's woods. Danny deserves a letter of commendation for his rescue. Working together as a group, draft a letter to Danny from the Secret Poachers' Society commending him on his heroism. Design a medal to accompany his commendation and display the medal and commendation for your classmates to see.

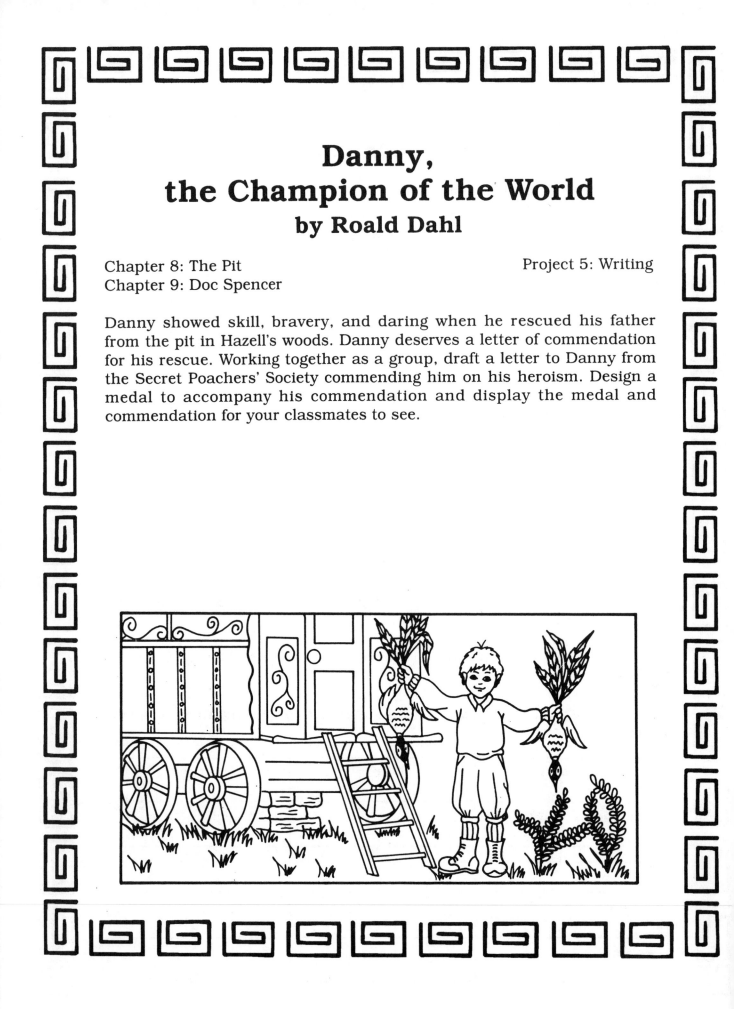

GA1425

# Danny,
# the Champion of the World
## by Roald Dahl

Chapter 10: The Great Shooting Party          Project 6: Handwriting
Chapter 11: The Sleeping Beauty

Mr. Victor Hazell spends all year preparing for his great shooting party. Pretend you are the printing company Mr. Hazell employs to make this year's invitations. Using your best handwriting, calligraphy and graphic designs, make this invitation. Include the time, date and any other information you feel is important.

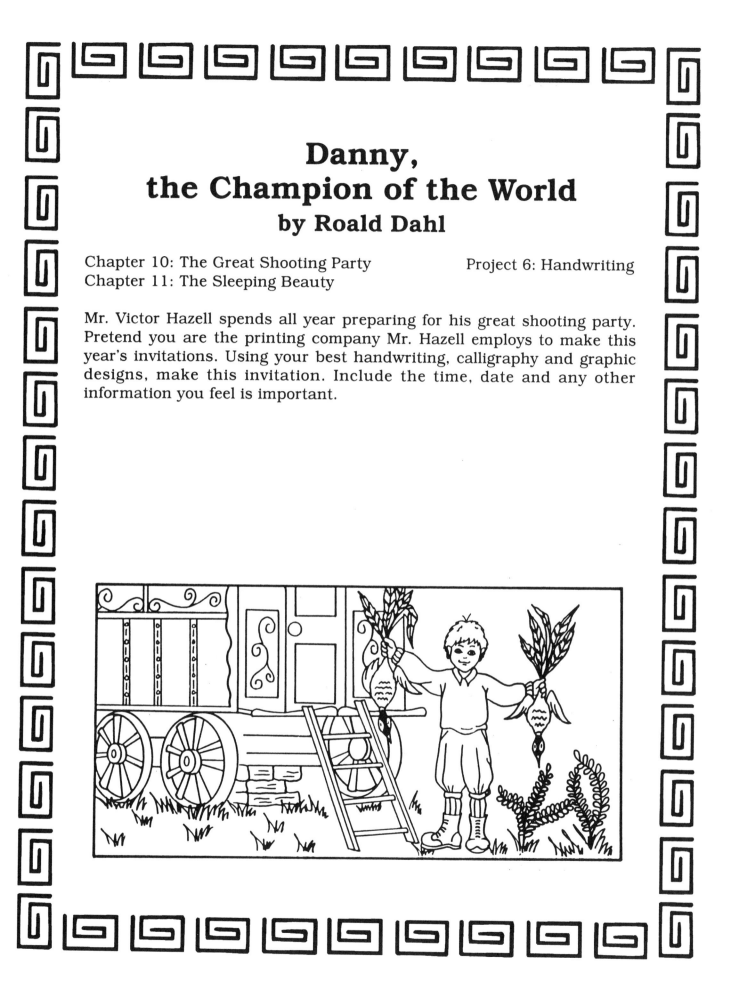

GA1425

# Danny,
# the Champion of the World
## by Roald Dahl

Chapter 12: Thursday and School     Project 7: Music
Chapter 13: Friday

Danny has a very close relationship with his father. In many ways they depend on each other. Using a popular melody, write and perform a song for the class about the close relationship between Danny and his father.

GA1425

# Danny,
# the Champion of the World
## by Roald Dahl

Chapter 14: In the Wood
Chapter 15: The Keeper

Project 8: Physical Challenge

Danny is a young boy who has a very close relationship with his father and is shocked when he discovers his father is a poacher. With the teacher's permission, carry out the following experiment, and then discuss with team members the questions below.

Place ten different objects on the teacher's desk and throughout the day see how many of these items you can "poach" from the desk. You may "poach" only one item at a time.

What is poaching? Why is it wrong to poach? Should you be punished for poaching? How severe should the punishment be?

GA1425

# Danny,
# the Champion of the World
## by Roald Dahl

Chapter 16: The Champion of the World              Project 9: Reading
Chapter 17: The Taxi

There is a book about a boy named Charlie that has some similarities to Danny. Read the last three chapters of *Charlie and the Chocolate Factory*. Compare the success of Danny and Charlie in these two very different, yet surprisingly similar books. Consider how each boy is thought of as a champion. As a team, list the similarities between Danny and Charlie. Continue working together to write a paragraph describing changes in the boys. Share your list and paragraph with your teacher.

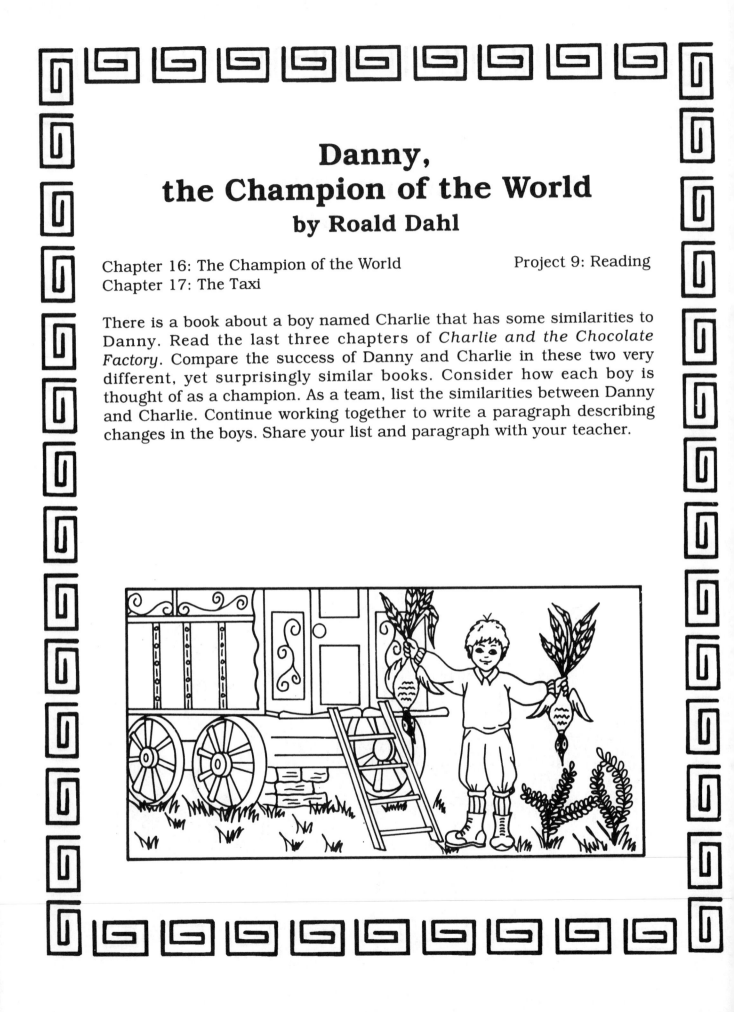

                                                                                          GA1425

# Danny,
# the Champion of the World
## by Roald Dahl

Chapter 18: Home
Chapter 19: Rockabye Baby

Project 10: Social Studies

Imagine! One hundred and twenty pheasants on one poaching expedition! As a group, do research on the pheasant. Prepare a fact sheet which will include the following information:

origin
varieties
size
appearance/coloring
nesting habits
food
uses to man

Post your fact sheet for your classmates to see.

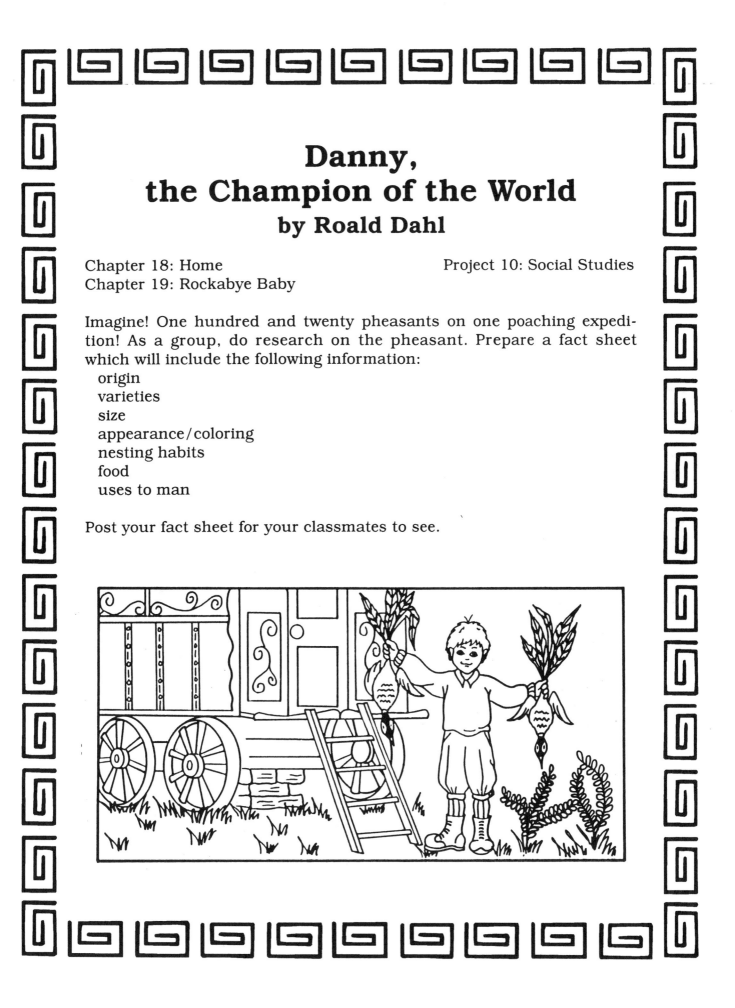

# Danny,
# the Champion of the World
## by Roald Dahl

Chapter 20: Good-bye Mr. Hazell                    Project 11: Drama

Use the dialogue from this chapter to create and perform a readers' theater or a skit about the pheasants, Mr. Hazell, Enoch Samways, Danny, his father and all others in this funny chapter. Rehearse and present it to the class.

GA1425

# Danny,
# the Champion of the World
## by Roald Dahl

Chapter 21: Doc Spencer's Surprise                    Project 12: Cooking
Chapter 22: My Father

Having enjoyed reading this book, you must realize how important raisins are to the story. Use this recipe to make your own raisins.

### Raisin Recipe*
(With adult supervision)

Place 2 cups (480 ml) of grapes on a cookie sheet and turn the oven on as low as possible. Shake the grapes every hour to rearrange them and allow them to dry evenly. Depending on the variety of grapes you choose, you can turn grapes into raisins in about 7 hours using a conventional oven. Raisins can be made in a shorter period of time if grapes are placed in a microwave oven for 3 minutes on "high" and then dried for 2 hours in a conventional oven on "low" (about 150°F [65.5°C]).

Have each member of the group make the above recipe and bring the raisins to class to share with your classmates.

*You'll probably like the raisins better if you start with seedless grapes.

GA1425

# The Westing Game
## by Ellen Raskin

Chapter 1: Sunset Towers

Chapter 2: Ghosts or Worse

Chapter 3: Tenants in and Out

Project 1: Art

In Chicago, the Sears Tower reaches 1454 feet (443.47 m) toward the sky. The CN Tower in Toronto, Canada, is the world's tallest self-supporting structure, climbing 1821 feet (552.37 m) skyward. Neither, however, could possibly hold the mystery the Sunset Towers contains in our book.

Using a large cardboard box, make a representation of the Sunset Towers. Place the correct families in their places; make thin cardboard cutouts of the inhabitants and put them in their apartments. If possible, make paper furnishings to add realism to your creation. Share the work and don't forget the doorman!

GA1425

# The Westing Game
## by Ellen Raskin

Chapter 4:  The Corpse Found
Chapter 5:  Sixteen Heirs

Project 2: Writing

To help keep your clues straight, create "character cards" (5" x 8" [12.7 x 20.32 cm] index cards) for each person introduced in the story. These will be used to record clues about each character. You will find the character cards, if kept current, will help you solve the "Westing Game." Compare your cards among your team members to share insights. Remember, not all "clues" are useful. (That sneaky author!) Share your cards with the teacher; then keep the cards with your book.

GA1425

# The Westing Game
## by Ellen Raskin

Chapter 6: The Westing Will        Project 3: Handwriting
Chapter 7: The Westing Game
Chapter 8: The Paired Heirs

Calligraphy is the fine art of handwriting. The ancient Persians and Chinese regarded calligraphy as an art form. Use butcher paper to make a calligraphy copy of the will. Post the finished product so the class can see it and you can refer to it often as you read *The Westing Game*. (Hint: The will holds an important clue for the solution.)

GA1425

# The Westing Game
## by Ellen Raskin

Chapter 9:  Lost and Found
Chapter 10: The Long Party

Project 4: Cooking

Judge Ford has a party catered by Mr. Shin Hoo. With adult/teacher supervision, make won-ton desserts for the class to enjoy. Follow the recipe below.

### Won-Ton Desserts

**Ingredients:**
  won-ton wrappers* (available in the frozen food sections of most
    supermarkets)
  cooking oil
  sugar
  cinnamon

**Other items needed:**
  frying pan
  tongs
  paper towels

Heat about 1/2" (1.25 cm) of the oil to 350°F (176°C). When oil is hot, fry the won-ton wrappers (a few at a time) until they are light brown in color. (Hot oil is very dangerous; make sure you are very careful and have an adult's supervision.) When browned lightly, use the tongs to remove the fried won-tons from the frying pan; drain the skins on paper toweling. (Westing super absorbant paper towels work best!) While still hot, sprinkle a mixture of sugar and cinnamon on top. Let them cool a few minutes before tasting them. They really taste great!

*If won-ton wrappers are not available locally, substitute very thin pie crust dough or tortillas.

GA1425

# The Westing Game
## by Ellen Raskin

Chapter 11: The Meeting
Chapter 12: The First Bomb
Chapter 13: The Second Bomb

Project 5: Math

The stock exchange is a marketplace for the buying and selling of stocks and bonds. Your local newspaper probably carries the transactions on the New York Stock Exchange. A study of the stock market is a fun and interesting way to study America. Allow each member of your team $1000 to spend on the stock(s) of his choice. You may buy as few or as many shares of stock as you choose; however, you must not purchase over $1000 worth in total.

Use a newspaper to make stock selections. At the end of one week "sell" your stocks and determine which team member made his $1000 grow the most.

Remember: "Buy Westing paper products."

GA1425

# The Westing Game
## by Ellen Raskin

Chapter 14: Pairs Repaired
Chapter 15: Fact and Gossip

Project 6: Drama

The "Who's on First" routine performed by Bud Abbott and Lou Costello is well-known and enjoyed by everyone. It gave Grace her idea for renaming Shin Hoo's restaurant. Obtain a copy of "Who's on First" and present the skit to the class. If you feel really talented, try to perform the routine without a script. Split your team so half plays Abbott's part and the other half plays Costello's role. Practice several days to get the timing and comedic delivery, and then present it to your classmates. Try your public library for a copy of this old-time tape or script.

If you are unsuccessful in obtaining a tape or script of "Who's on First," substitute a readers' theater production of the driveway scene near the beginning of Chapter 15.

GA1425

# The Westing Game
## by Ellen Raskin

Chapter 16: The Third Bomb                    Project 7: Science
Chapter 17: Some Solutions
Chapter 18: The Trackers

FAMOUS INVENTORS, PLEASE REGISTER HERE!

James Hoo invented paper innersoles after the suggestion by Sandy McSouthers. Put on your thinking caps and invent something that can be worn. Your inventions (one per team member) can be very practical (like innersoles) or fashion oriented. Wear your creations to class when completed.

GA1425

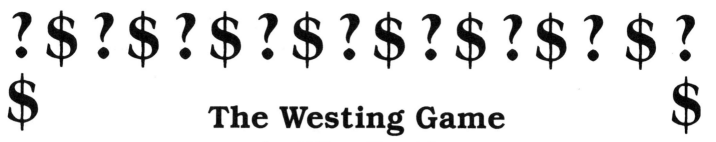

# The Westing Game
## by Ellen Raskin

Chapter 19: Odd Relatives

Chapter 20: Confessions

Project 8: Social Studies

Have you ever tried to read a menu written in a foreign language? Sometimes you can't tell if you're ordering antelope or artichokes.

Help Shin Hoo by making a new menu for his restaurant. You may want to use pictures and illustrations to make your menu "come to life." It's okay to "borrow" ideas from other menus you've seen. Try to include some Chinese writing on your menu.

143

# The Westing Game
## by Ellen Raskin

Chapter 21: The Fourth Bomb

Chapter 22: Losers, Winners

Chapter 23: Strange Answers

Project 9: Physical Challenge

Doug Hoo hopes one day to compete in the Olympics. Design a simple "Westing Game Olympics" for your classmates. Suggested events might include the crutch run, hair (or yarn) braiding, chess playing, etc. You may choose to make your "olympics" an indoor event or an outdoor event. When you've designed your "olympics," challenge other teams to beat your team's collective "time" on the events.

# The Westing Game
## by Ellen Raskin

Chapter 24: Wrong All Wrong
Chapter 25: Westing's Wake

Project 10: Music

"God Bless America"; "America, the Beautiful"; "You're a Grand Old Flag"; and "The Star-Spangled Banner" were just some of Samuel Westing's favorite songs. Exactly which patriotic song was Westing's favorite remains a puzzle. Speaking of puzzles, have each team member choose a patriotic song that Sam Westing would have liked, and do the following:

Write out the lyrics for the chorus of the song and then carefully "cut them up" and challenge your teammates to work together to put the clues back in the correct order. When your teammates have correctly identified and reconstructed the song, glue it together on a separate sheet of paper and show it to your teacher.

GA1425

# The Westing Game
## by Ellen Raskin

Chapter 26: Turtle's Trial
Chapter 27: A Happy Fourth
Chapter 28: And Then...

Project 11: Reading

Solving a mystery before the author explains it to us always makes us feel like great detectives. One of the greatest detectives in literature was Sherlock Holmes. You may enjoy reading one of the chronicles of Mr. Sherlock Holmes written by Sir Conan Doyle. Holmes was known for his astute observation skills and ability to spot clues.

From *The Westing Game*, list ten clues that should have led you to discovering the solution to the "game." You may need to reread parts of the book. Compare your list to the lists of your other team members.

GA1425

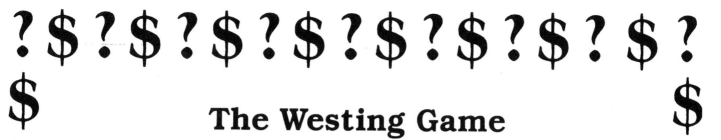

# The Westing Game
## by Ellen Raskin

Chapter 29: Five Years Pass
Chapter 30: The End?

Project 12: Language

It is possible to have a different ending to the story than the one written by the author.

Have each team member write a one-page epilogue that has a different winner than the one in the book. Compare and contrast your individual endings and decide, as a team, on which ending you prefer. Let your teacher know which ending your team prefers.

147

GA1425

# Sing Down the Moon
## by Scott O'Dell

Chapters 1-2                                    Project 1: Cooking

In this Indian saga, obtaining food is a common thread throughout the book. Since the Indians didn't have refrigeration, they had to gather food in times of plenty and store it by drying it. This drying process turned meat into jerky. Follow the recipe to make your own jerky to share with your classmates.

### Beef Jerky Recipe*

**Ingredients:**
  2 to 3 lbs. (.9 to 1.35 kg) of very thinly sliced beef
  bottle of teriyaki sauce
  salt and pepper

**Other items:**
  cookie sheets
  tongs
  paper towels

*Be sure to have a parent or teacher help out with the cooking. Be careful of hot cookie sheets!

After marinating beef strips in teriyaki sauce for one hour, blot beef dry with paper towels and lightly salt and pepper to taste. (Try some crushed hot peppers for those with a daring spirit and a cast iron stomach.)

Place the strips in a single layer on a cookie sheet and place in an oven set on its lowest setting (about 150°F [65.6°C]). Turn the beef strips every hour until they are dry and leathery to the touch. Drying time will vary according to the thickness of the meat strips, but the meat should be done in 3 to 4 hours.

Store dried jerky in plastic bags and treat your class members to an Indian delight.

GA1425

# Sing Down the Moon
## by Scott O'Dell

Chapters 3-4                                                 Project 2: Music

Music and dancing accompanied many Indian ceremonies. Many tribes used rattles, clappers, and drums to accompany their songs and chants. A visit to your local library may give you some insight into some of the simple chants and songs sung by our Native Americans.

Work together as a team to create an Indian chant. After practicing your chant (complete with drums), apply tempera paint to each other's faces (carefully and sparingly) and present your Indian chant to your class.

GA1425

# Sing Down the Moon
## by Scott O'Dell

Chapters 5-6                                      Project 3: Science

The Indians were very closely attuned to nature. They had legends about the stars as well as other natural phenomena. Each member of your team will make a North Star chart "tube" which will enable them to use the Big Dipper to find the North Star.

Using a potato chip canister, the center cardboard roll from paper towels or gift wrap, or rolled up construction paper, make a North Star chart "tube." Cover both ends of the canister with black construction paper. Make a slit about 1/2" x 1" (1.25 x 2.54 cm) into which you will look. At the other end of the canister use a straight pin or paper clip to poke holes in the construction paper to reproduce the Big Dipper. Note the proportions closely, then carefully make the North Star hole slightly larger than the "stars" of the Big Dipper. Compare your canister "road map" to the North Star to the real thing. Let your classmates use your chart to find the North Star (called Polaris).

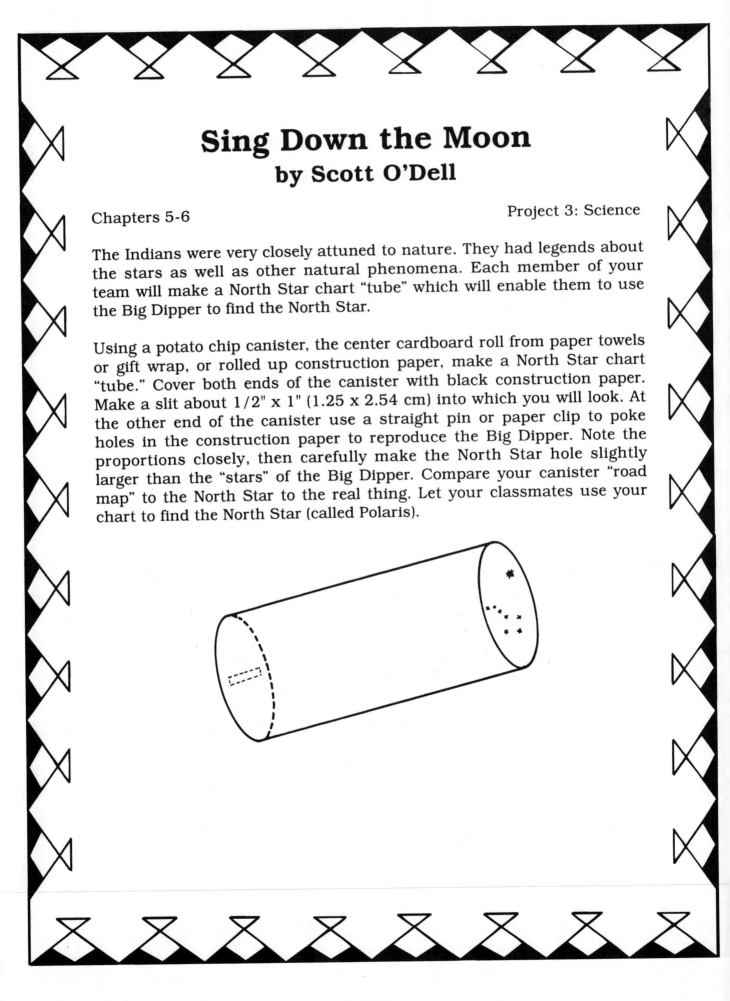

GA1425

# Sing Down the Moon
## by Scott O'Dell

Chapters 7-8                                            Project 4: Social Studies

The collective term *Indians* does not do justice to the diversity of our Native American population. Have each member of your team research a different Native American tribe. (Several different tribes are mentioned in *Sing Down the Moon*.) When complete, give an oral presentation to your class about the similarities and differences of the tribes. Topics to discuss include family life, government, housing and other structures, warfare, arts and crafts, religion, trade, and language. Also, be able to discuss the tribe as it is today. (Your teacher may suggest you write a written report in lieu of an oral presentation.)

                                                                GA1425

# Sing Down the Moon
## by Scott O'Dell

Chapters 9-10                                    Project 5: Drama

In *Sing Down the Moon*, Scott O'Dell uses very little dialogue; he tells the story using the narrative first person format. The early Native Americans had many different languages used by the different tribes. Because of the language differences, many tribes often used sign language when trading or communicating with someone outside their own tribe.

Working together as a team, "tell" the story of Bright Morning's capture using a form of sign language. Without words, present this story to your class and, when finished, ask them to recount the story in words to see how well you "signed" to them.

                                    GA1425

# Sing Down the Moon
## by Scott O'Dell

Chapters 11-12            Project 6: Handwriting

Many different cultures have ceremonies to honor a girl's entry into womanhood. These "coming out" parties are usually festive occasions with an underlying sense of appreciation of a particular ethnic or cultural group. Each member of your team is to create a modern invitation to a party honoring a member of your class. Use your best handwriting, possibly even calligraphy, on the cover of the invitation.

     GA1425

# Sing Down the Moon
## by Scott O'Dell

Chapters 13-14

Project 7: Art

Indian blankets have become collectors' items with many selling for thousands of dollars. After doing a little simple research, your team is to design and color an Indian blanket on a large sheet of butcher paper. Display the results for the class to see.

# Sing Down the Moon
## by Scott O'Dell

Chapters 15-16                    Project 8: Physical Challenge

An Indian game, lacrosse, is still played today. Try this modified game of lacrosse.

First collect a plastic quart or 2-liter beverage container for each player. (Suggestion: 6 players per team.) Carefully cut off the bottom of the bottle and wash out the top of the container. Using a tennis ball, and catching and throwing it only with the container, run and pass the ball to other members of your team. When you are close enough, "throw" the ball between your opponent's goal. (Remember, you can't touch the ball with your hands.)

If you are touched while you have the ball in your container, you must give the ball to your opponent, and all members of your team must move away 15 feet (4.55 m). Your opponent will start the play by trying to advance the ball toward your goal. The game is to be played much like soccer (without contact between players). You may run and pass at will, but may not go out of bounds or touch the ball with your "free" hand.

The field should be set up as follows:

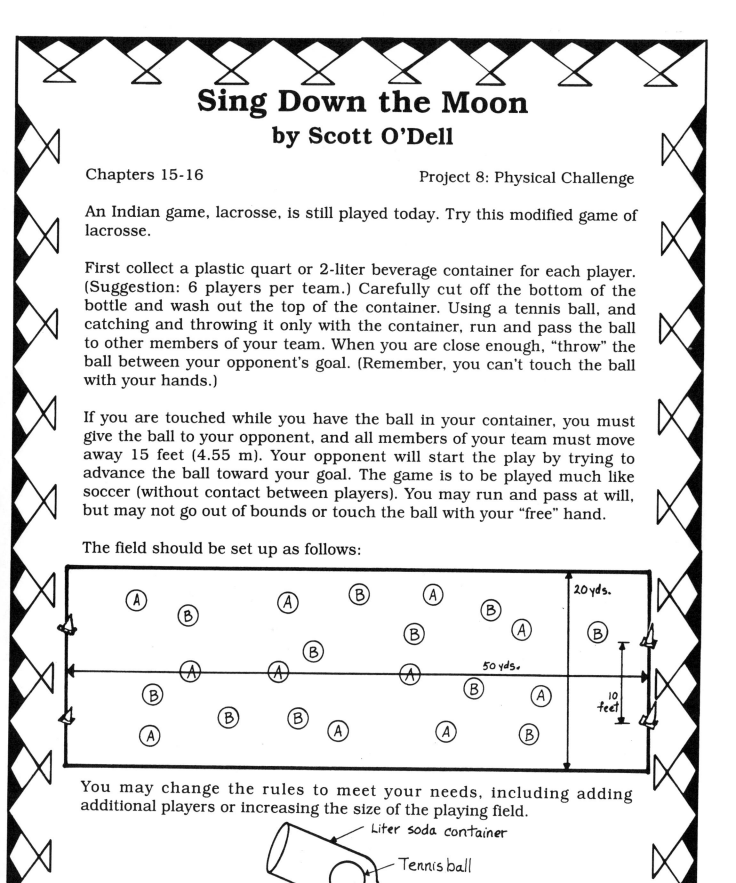

Liter soda container
Tennis ball

You may change the rules to meet your needs, including adding additional players or increasing the size of the playing field.

GA1425

# Sing Down the Moon
## by Scott O'Dell

Chapters 17-18                                      Project 9: Reading

The Long Walk forced on the Navajos may have made you feel that they had been treated unfairly. This "rounding up" of the Navajos is historically accurate and was led by Colonel Kit Carson, another famous name in American history.

Unfortunately, the Navajos were not the only Indian tribe unjustly treated by the American government. History records many broken treaties and injustices inflicted upon our Native Americans. A tragic episode in America's history is the movement of the Five Civilized Tribes and their Trail of Tears.

Read and research the Cherokee and Choctaw Trail of Tears. Compare the Long Walk of the Navajos to Bosque Redondo (Fort Sumner) with that of the Cherokee Trail of Tears. Give an oral presentation to the class about the treatment of our Native Americans by the government during this time period.

GA1425

# Sing Down the Moon
## by Scott O'Dell

Chapters 19-20                                    Project 10: Writing

Bright Morning and her family suffer many hardships at Bosque Redondo. She is surrounded by people who have "given up."

Each team member is to write a letter of hope and encouragement to Bright Morning explaining his support and giving her courage to continue. Post your letters for classmates to see.

GA1425

# Sing Down the Moon
## by Scott O'Dell

Chapters 21-22

Project 11: Language

Apache, Spanish, Navajo, Nez Percé, English, Zuni, and Kiowa are all languages mentioned in the book. Make a list of at least ten words from as many of these sources as possible. Post this list with their English translations for your class to view.

# Sing Down the Moon
## by Scott O'Dell

Chapter 23 and Postscript

Project 12: Math

Sheep are an important asset to the Navajo Indians, providing meat and wool. Suppose Tall Boy and Bright Morning can find six of their original sheep, of which two are rams. Suppose that one-half of the sheep have twins and the other half have one lamb per sheep per year. If the couple loses two lambs per year to coyotes, and it takes two full years for the sheep to grow to maturity, how many sheep will they have at the end of two years?

GA1425

# Johnny Tremain
## by Esther Forbes

Chapter 1: Up and About        Project 1: Language

Show time!

Divide your team into two even groups. Each team selects ten vocabulary words from Chapter 1 and does not show them to the other group. Using a Password format, each team challenges the other to say the chosen word.

**Directions:**
Sit opposite the members of your team. Select one of the vocabulary words from your opponent's list. Using one-word clues, try to get your teammate to guess the word. If your first teammate guesses correctly on your first clue, you receive ten points. If your first teammate's response is wrong, you give another one-word clue to your second teammate. A correct answer is now worth nine points. Each guess is worth one point less until either your teammates have guessed correctly or you have given ten clues. Your teammates may answer with only a one-word response.

Your opponents follow the same procedure using the words your team has selected. Keep score to determine a winner.

     GA1425

# Johnny Tremain
## by Esther Forbes

Chapter 2: The Pride of Your Power          Project 2: Music

"Yankee Doodle" was one of the songs to come out of the Revolutionary War. Research another song that was popular during the Revolutionary War period. Pass out copies of the song to classmates and teach the song to them.

GA1425

# Johnny Tremain
## by Esther Forbes

Chapter 3: An Earth of Brass                    Project 3: Art

In the days of Johnny Tremain it was not unusual to find people who could not read or write. Because so many people could not read, shop owners hung signs over the door representing their businesses. A pair of scissors represented a tailor, a gold lamb represented a wool weaver, a compass was for an instrument maker, etc.

Having read Chapter 3, each member of your group is to make two picture signs that represent two different businesses. Post these completed signs where the class can view them. See if your classmates can guess what kind of business each sign represents.

GA1425

# Johnny Tremain
## by Esther Forbes

Chapter 4: The Rising Eye

Project 4: Writing

As a group, write a front page for the *Boston Observer* newspaper. Be sure to include a headline as well as a title banner with the name of the paper. Include articles you might have found in Johnny's time. Possible articles might include a lost pig..., Johnny Tremain cleared in court..., barn raising held..., British soldiers continue to be stationed in Boston..., ship arrives..., and other articles your own imagination can provide.

Cut and paste together the articles in such a way that it looks like a newspaper, and use a copy machine to put together the final copy which you will post for your classmates to see.

GA1425

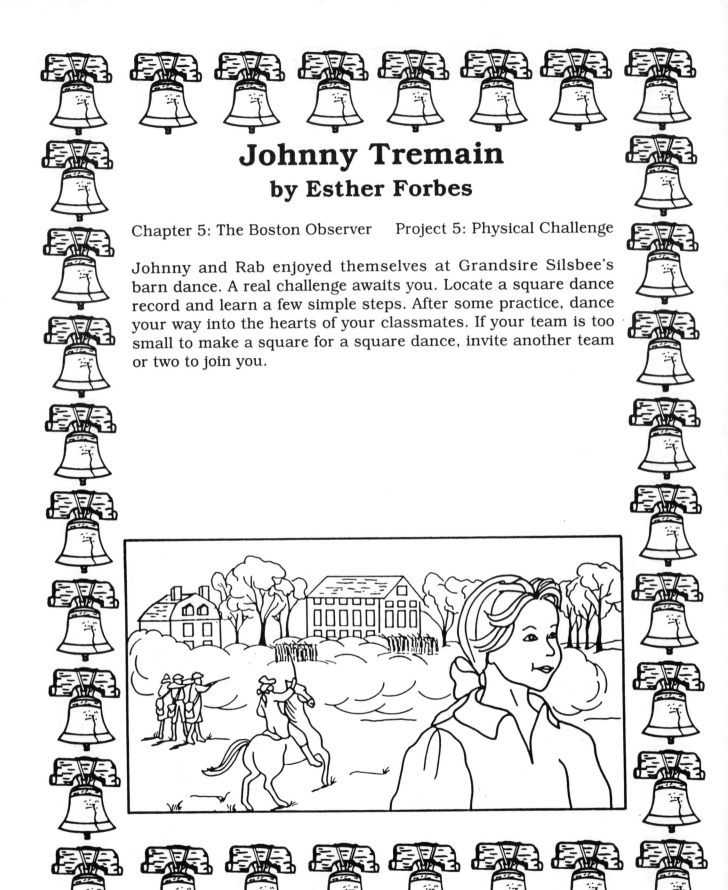

# Johnny Tremain
## by Esther Forbes

Chapter 5: The Boston Observer    Project 5: Physical Challenge

Johnny and Rab enjoyed themselves at Grandsire Silsbee's barn dance. A real challenge awaits you. Locate a square dance record and learn a few simple steps. After some practice, dance your way into the hearts of your classmates. If your team is too small to make a square for a square dance, invite another team or two to join you.

GA1425

# Johnny Tremain
## by Esther Forbes

Chapter 6: Salt-Water Tea        Project 6: Social Studies

The Boston Tea Party has been recorded in history as one of the events that led to the Revolutionary War in America. Research the Boston Tea Party...its causes and results. Dress like a band of "Yankee Indians" and explain the events surrounding the Tea Party to your classmates.

GA1425

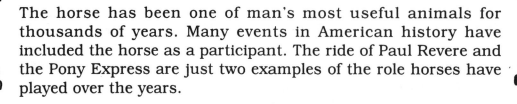

# Johnny Tremain
## by Esther Forbes

Chapter 7: The Fiddler's Bill                    Project 7: Science

The horse has been one of man's most useful animals for thousands of years. Many events in American history have included the horse as a participant. The ride of Paul Revere and the Pony Express are just two examples of the role horses have played over the years.

Johnny Tremain's horse, Goblin, was Johnny's pride and joy. Working as a group and dividing the work evenly, prepare a report on horses. Discuss the different kinds of horses, their uses, origins, anatomy, and types of riding equipment. Your report should also include the role of horses in history with emphasis on American events in which the horse was an important participant.

# Johnny Tremain
## by Esther Forbes

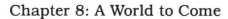

Chapter 8: A World to Come                    Project 8: Drama

Chapter 8 contains a stirring speech by James Otis. He questions the reasons for war and puts it in a powerfully simple statement, "Only that a man can stand up." Choose parts according to the book and practice this James Otis speech. In addition to Otis, your team will need people to play the parts of Rab, Sam Adams, Johnny, Joseph Warren, John Hancock, Paul Revere, and John Adams. It may be necessary for some team members to play two roles.

Using a tape recorder, prepare and practice the James Otis speech. Include appropriate background sounds and rehearse your delivery to get the mood and feeling of the men who were called traitors by some, patriots by others. If you desire, you may wish to present this speech in readers' theater form.

167

GA1425

# Johnny Tremain
## by Esther Forbes

Chapter 9: The Scarlet Deluge          Project 9: Handwriting

How do I love thee, let me count the ways....

When writing a love letter one must be very careful to use only the finest, fanciest paper and his best penmanship. Selecting the most "special" paper available and using calligraphy writing, make a copy of the letter written by Lieutenant Stranger to Miss Lavinia Lyte. Post this partial love letter for your class to view. Perhaps those of you smitten by the "love bug" can even finish the letter or pen a reply.

GA1425

# Johnny Tremain
## by Esther Forbes

Chapter 10: Disperse, Ye Rebels!        Project 10: Reading

Although the book is called *Johnny Tremain*, I'm sure you recognized the name of Paul Revere as well as many other famous persons brought to life by this book. Read the poem "The Midnight Ride of Paul Revere," by Henry Wadsworth Longfellow. Read this poem together into a tape recorder and play it for the class to hear.

GA1425

# Johnny Tremain
## by Esther Forbes

Chapter 11: Yankee Doodle                    Project 11: Math

The Redcoats had a tremendous force of soldiers in Boston.
Answer the following: Suppose the British had 1200 men in
Boston. If each of these men had 6 buttons on his blouse
(military shirt) and every tenth man rode a horse and 19 out of
20 men had a musket, how many muskets, buttons, and
horseshoes did the British have in Boston?

GA1425

# Johnny Tremain
## by Esther Forbes

Chapter 12: A Man Can Stand Up          Project 12: Cooking

As the war raged on and the British squeezed off Boston's new supplies, people had to count on their "stores" of food they had saved. Try this recipe for dried apples.

### Dried Apples
(Caution: Have an adult/parent supervise as you make this recipe.)

1. Wash, peel, and remove the core of four or five apples.
2. Carefully slice the apples into 1/4" (.6 cm) slices.
3. Wrinkle a sheet of aluminum foil and lay it on the bottom of a cookie sheet. (The wrinkles let the air circulate to dry the apples more quickly.)
4. Place the apples in an oven at the oven's lowest setting (between 150 and 200°F [65.5 and 93.3°C]).
5. Turn the slices every hour until they are dried and leathery (about 2-3 hours).

Since apples are 84 percent water, it may not be possible to completely dry the apples in one day. If this is the case, cover them with a clean cloth and continue the process the second day. The dried apple slices will turn brown but are fine to eat. Eat all of them in a day or so, or refrigerate the "apple jerky."

Share your apple "jerky" with your classmates...yummy!

GA1425

# Analysis Pages

GA1425

Name _____

Date _____

# The Secret of the Indian
## by Lynne Reid Banks

It all started when Omri discovered he could bring to life the miniature plastic Indian, the American cowboy and other toy figures. But after a year Omri never would have guessed that it would start all over again! The responsibilities of food and shelter for his tiny friends and the enormous stress that grown-ups would discover the unbelievable scene in his room were too much for Omri. The fact that new people find out about the magic in Omri's room and the incredible transport of Patrick and Omri back to the old American West add suspense to the story.

People die while others teeter on the brink of death. When and how will it all stop without disrupting the past history of the world? The book is filled with realism as the reader is caught up in the turmoil that grows and grows in Omri's attic bedroom.

1. Imagine you have the secret of the cupboard. How long could you keep the secret from adults, and with whom would you share the secret?

2. If you could time travel just one time, what period in history would you like to visit and why?

3. Do you think it is possible that plastic figures could come alive? Give your reasons.

4. Suppose a robber came through the window in your house. What would you do?

5. Who has the most creative imagination in *The Secret of the Indian*? Give reasons for your answer.

6. How would you feel if the principal read your award-winning paper to the entire school?

7. Rate *The Secret of the Indian* from 1 to 10 with 10 being the best.

8. Which project did your group enjoy most?

9. How are Omri and Patrick alike?

10. Did your team work well as a group? Give some examples for your opinion.

Name _____

Date _____

# The Lion, the Witch and the Wardrobe
## by C.S. Lewis

The adventures of Narnia begin with an innocent peek into a wardrobe that changes the lives of four children forever. The perils of adventure engulf the children as they return to Narnia through the soft warm furs that turn into rough cold tree branches. They are faced with overpowering the White Witch and saving a kingdom, but one of them is a traitor. Who could it be? Battles are waged and fought as creatures turn into stone for many years. Only one can return and save the kingdom. But is it too late? Can Narnia be saved? With willpower, determination and devotion, many fight against evil but is it enough? Isn't right supposed to conquer in the end?

1. After reading *The Lion, the Witch and the Wardrobe*, how do you feel about brothers and sisters sticking together?

2. The characters in Narnia kept asking the children if they were human. How would you classify the characters in Narnia?

3. If you and your team had found the wardrobe, who would have gone through to Narnia? Why did you choose that person(s)?

4. If there is a hero in this book, who would it be and why did you choose that one as the hero?

5. If the Professor, the owner of the house, knew that the wardrobe led to such a dangerous adventure, why did he allow the children to explore the wardrobe?

GA1425

6. Do the lion and the witch from Narnia remind you of any other characters or people you have read about in other books? If so, who?

7. Rate *The Lion, the Witch and the Wardrobe* from 1 to 10 with 10 being the best.

8. Which project did your group enjoy most?

9. How do you feel about the witch's quest for Narnia?

10. Did your team work well as a group? Give some examples for your opinion.

Name _____

Date _____

# Mrs. Frisby and the Rats of NIMH
## by Robert C. O'Brien

Mrs. Frisby, an uncommon field mouse, is faced with a dilemma. Farmer Fitzgibbon would soon "plow under" Mrs. Frisby's winter home. With the illness of Timothy, her young son, moving becomes a matter of life and death.

Help from a very special group of rats, an encounter with Dragon (the fierce cat), and a very cunning plan are all woven together into this 1972 Newbery Medal story of friendship, skill, cleverness, and adventure. The National Institute of Mental Health (NIMH) will never be the same!

1. Why do you suppose that Jonathan did not tell Mrs. Frisby about NIMH and the rats?
2. Rats that can read and use tools? C'mon now...yet this book of fantasy was very believable. How did the author make the story seem so realistic?
3. What happened to the rats while they were at NIMH that made them special?
4. Pretend you are Nicodemus and the time is several years later. Do you feel you would still want to write about your adventures? How could you write it so people would believe it? Explain.
5. Rate *Mrs. Frisby and the Rats of NIMH* from 1 to 10 with 10 being the best.
6. Mr. O'Brien created very strong characterizations in this story. Select your favorite character and describe him/her.
7. Do you think it is now possible, or will ever be possible, to create "super rats" or "super anythings" that will have the ability to think like humans?
8. If it were possible to create as dramatic a change in humans as those changes described in the rats, how would that affect the world?
9. Which project did your group enjoy most?
10. The rats, Mrs. Frisby, and the owl all knew the value of teamwork. In what way did your group demonstrate teamwork?

Name _____

Date _____

# The Secret Garden
## by Frances Hodgson Burnett

Mary is an unhappy orphan that is forced to live in the English home of a wealthy uncle, a man who has made no time for children since the untimely death of his wife who died during childbirth. There is a mysterious young boy found in the mansion who reigns over everyone but Mary. Secrets and other mysterious people run wild throughout this book. Mary finds a secret garden on the grounds that has been hidden in the minds of the old gardener and Mary's uncle for years. Life changes for all who become entangled with Mary's temperament and will to see things grow. Startling changes come over many of the characters in this book who are touched in some way by the secret garden.

1. Describe Mary's attitude when she lived in India.

2. What made Mary's attitude change in England?

3. Suppose Mary and Colin had never met, what do you think would have happened to Colin?

4. Predict what Dickon will do for a living and describe what it might be.

5. Explain why Mr. Craven spent so little time at Misselthwaite Manor?

6. How would you have dealt with a screaming, temper-tantrum-throwing Colin?

7. Rate *The Secret Garden* from 1 to 10 with 10 being the best.

8. Which project did your group enjoy most?

9. Compare and contrast Mary's life and Dickon's life?

10. Did your team work well as a group? Give some examples for your opinion.

GA1425

Name _____

Date _____

# The Cay
## by Theodore Taylor

German submarines threaten the lives of the people on Curacao, a Dutch island off the coast of Venezuela in 1942. A young boy, Phillip, and his mother leave the island but disaster hits the fleeing vessel. A shipwrecked Phillip shows his prejudices as he refuses help from Timothy, an old boat hand. As his life continues to depend on Timothy, Phillip learns that being blind can truly open one's mind. Phillip and Timothy struggle through natural and emotional disasters that make them both stronger in one sense and one of them weaker as death draws near. *The Cay* is a wonderful story of young and old, black and white and learning from each other. Some of the heartaches of survival are overcome while others are too enormous to comprehend.

1. Why was Phillip's mother so concerned about leaving the country at the beginning of the book?

2. Describe Phillip's first impression of Timothy and compare it to his feelings of Timothy by the end of the book.

3. If you were stranded on an island for an uncertain length of time with someone you thought you hated, how would you handle the situation?

4. Imagine you were Phillip's parents. What would you have done to locate Phillip?

5. What sort of a person was Timothy?

6. What was the most important thing Phillip learned while on the island?

GA1425

7. Rate *The Cay* from 1 to 10 with 10 being the best.

8. Which project did your group enjoy most?

9. Predict what would have happened to Phillip if he would have had to stay on the island another thirty days by himself.

10. Did your team work well as a group? Give some examples for your opinion.

GA1425

# Where the Red Fern Grows
## by Wilson Rawls

This book is an unforgettable story of love and devotion between a boy and his dogs. Billy worked hard for the day when he could have his hounds. He and his dogs were rarely parted as they night hunted the old hills and river bottoms of the beautiful Ozarks. Billy, Old Dan, and Little Ann were known across the hills and valleys as the hunting trio to beat. Some tried and failed, but in the end something else won out to the heartache of Billy. His family had commitments to keep, so life had to go on. This is an exciting tale of love and adventure that is magical in so many ways. The ending of this book is mixed with sadness and happiness that represents the end of lives and the beginning of others' lives.

1. Billy wanted a dog more than anything else in the world. Has there ever been something you wanted that much; if so, explain.

2. Describe how you felt when Billy and his dogs won the raccoon hunt.

3. Who do you think Billy was closest to, besides his dogs? Justify your answer.

4. Judge how you would have felt if it had been you with Rubin Pritchard when he died.

5. What if Billy had never gotten his dogs? How do you suppose Billy would have gone raccoon hunting?

GA1425

6. Explain your interpretation of the red fern that grew between the dogs' graves.

7. Rate *Where the Red Fern Grows* from 1 to 10 with 10 being the best.

8. Which project did your group enjoy most?

9. Predict what would have happened to Billy's dogs had they not died when they moved out of the mountains.

10. Did your team work well as a group? Give some examples for your opinion.

# From the Mixed-Up Files of Mrs. Basil E. Frankweiler
## by E.L. Konigsburg

Claudia is unhappy with life at home and feels unappreciated. Desiring a change, Claudia enlists the help of Jamie, her penny-pinching younger brother, and together they have a "running way" adventure unlike any other. Living at the Metropolitan Museum of Art, they encounter an exhibit surrounded by mystery. Add to this mixture Mrs. Basil E. Frankweiler, a somewhat eccentric and very rich old lady who is at the center of the mystery, and you have a charming story about family relationships, changes, and growing up that will delight the reader.

1. Everyone at one time or another has the feeling that he is not appreciated. What are the ways you feel you're not appreciated? (Be honest.) How do you deal with your feelings?
2. Why was Jamie such a good complement to Claudia for this adventure?
3. Claudia chose an art museum in a crowded city as her "running to" place. Would you have chosen the same kind of place or somewhere different? If you would choose a different place, describe your place and why you would choose it.
4. Mrs. Basil E. Frankweiler knew more about the children than they knew. How?
5. Although we never see or hear from the lawyer Saxonberg, Mrs. Frankweiler's notes and chronicles give us a fair amount of insight into his personality. Describe the lawyer Saxonberg and explain his role and relationship to Claudia and Jamie, Mrs. Frankweiler, and the story.
6. Rate this book on a scale of 1 to 10 with 10 being the best.
7. Which project did your group enjoy most?
8. Did you "see" any of yourself or your problems in this story? Explain.
9. If you had been the author, how would you have changed some of the characters in the book?
10. Working as a team has many benefits. Claudia and Jamie demonstrated teamwork. How did your group members demonstrate teamwork?

# A Wrinkle in Time
## by Madeleine L'Engle

This book is a combination of science fiction, mystery, suspense and horror that starts off with the arrival of a most disturbing stranger. Meg Murry's father has been missing for some time and people have formed many opinions and started dozens of rumors about his disappearance. But Meg never gives up hope that he will return. When the opportunity to go and find him arises, Meg and her intuitive brother "fly" at the chance to investigate. Little did they know just how far out they would travel. A new concept of a tesseract is explored by the human beings with not so human others as their guides. This Newbery Medal winner is hard to put down!

1. If you had been the children's neighbors and been able to watch some of the things that were going on at their house, how would you describe the strange happenings?
2. What do you think the children's father was involved with to have taken him so far from home?
3. There was a special bond between Meg and Charles Wallace. It seems as though he could read her mind. Do you know anyone who has these or other special talents? Explain your person's talents.
4. Summarize the feeling that prevailed over everyone in the place where they found their father.
5. Who is your favorite character in *A Wrinkle in Time* and why?
6. Explain whether you think it is right to tesseract.
7. Rate *A Wrinkle in Time* from 1 to 10 with 10 being the best.
8. Which project did your group enjoy most?
9. Predict what would have happened to their father if the children had not found him.
10. Did your team work well as a group? Give some examples for your opinion.

GA1425

# Danny,
## the Champion of the World
### by Roald Dahl

Danny is a young boy with a great treasure, a dad who is "Sparky." When Danny discovers his dad is a poacher (as is just about everyone in the district), he is shocked. This shock turns to enthusiasm when Danny discovers a way to help turn Mr. Victor Hazell's ill-famed pheasant shooting party into a farce. With the help of the doctor, the local constable, the Vicker's wife and, of course, his beloved dad, Danny proves himself as the "champion of the world."

1. Describe the relationship between Danny and his father.

2. What does the Big Friendly Giant do with bad dreams?

3. Mr. Dahl creates within us a dislike for Mr. Victor Hazell. Explain how Mr. Hazell's treatment of Danny and his father add to your pleasure at the outcome of the story.

4. How did Danny's rescue of his dad show bravery and maturity?

5. What portion of *Danny, the Champion of the World* did you think was the funniest?

6. After Danny's success, how do you think the other people of the village treated him?

7. Compare the personality of Captain Lancaster to the personality of Mr. Victor Hazell.

8. Rate this book on a scale of 1 to 10 with 10 being the best.

9. Which project did your group enjoy most?

10. How did your group demonstrate team work while working on your projects?

# The Westing Game
## by Ellen Raskin

This exciting mystery pits the reader against the multimillionaire Samuel W. Westing. The characters and the clues are woven into a brilliant tapestry of mystery, adventure, and intrigue. Sixteen players are possible heirs to Sam Westing's fortune. The sum of $200,000,000 is at stake in this "part mystery story, part play-along game, and part do-it-yourself puzzle." This 1978 Newbery Medal winner is delicious reading.

1. Explain how Mrs. Wexler treats Angela differently than she does Turtle. How does this help explain Turtle's behavior?

2. Ellen Raskin "loads up" the reader with lots of clues. The difficulty is determining which information is important and which is not. List several "clues" that the author purposely places to mislead the reader.

3. What relationship did Crow have to Sam Westing?

4. Why did Angela set the bombs?

5. Which of Sam Westing's characters do you feel were the closest to the real Samuel Westing?

6. At the end of the book, the death of Julian R. Eastman has an emotional impact on T.R. Wexler. How did Eastman's death affect you? Explain.

7. This game/puzzle/mystery book is a mixture of different types of books. Explain why it could be called a game/puzzle/mystery book and which of these descriptions do you feel best fits the story?

8. Rate *The Westing Game* on a scale of 1 to 10 with 10 being the best.

9. Which project did your group enjoy most?

10. How did your group use teamwork to solve your problems?

Name _____

Date _____

# Sing Down the Moon
## by Scott O'Dell

Bright Morning, a young Navajo girl, lives a relatively tranquil life in Canyon de Chelly. This tranquility is shattered by Spanish slavers, white soldiers, and a long, devastating march to Fort Sumner.

Bright Morning's story is one of bravery as well as broken spirits, hope as well as broken promises, and the inner strength of one girl longing to return to her native way of life. The story shows us injustices through the sometimes stoic eyes of one whose human spirit cannot be broken.

1. After reading *Sing Down the Moon*, how do you feel about the treatment received by the Native Americans of that time period at the hands of the American government?
2. The Indians at Canyon de Chelly seemed self-sufficient. How did this self-sufficiency change at Bosque Redondo?
3. In Navajo culture the woman owns the property and holds a unique position in the society. How is this different from your culture, and what are your feelings about it?
4. This story takes place in 1864. What events were transpiring in the rest of America at about this same time?
5. Bright Morning expressed very little emotion in the story. It is written in a very matter-of-fact manner with little in the way of extra descriptions. Do you feel this added to the realism of the story or detracted from its emotional impact?
6. Rate *Sing Down the Moon* from 1 to 10 with 10 being the best.
7. *Sing Down the Moon* is just one of Scott O'Dell's books about young people dealing with adversity. Compare this book to any other books you may have read by this Newbery Medal-winning author.
8. Do you believe that there are any groups of people treated similarly by our government today? If so, which group(s)?
9. Which project did your group enjoy most?
10. The Native Americans learned that working together was necessary for the benefit of all. How did your group demonstrate teamwork?

GA1425

Name _____

Date _____

# Johnny Tremain
## by Esther Forbes

Johnny Tremain, a young silversmith, gets caught up in the turbulent pre-Revolutionary War times of Boston. Following a terrible burn he receives on his hand, Johnny finds his lifelong occupation and desire suddenly stripped from him. After a period of adjustment he meets Rab, a confident young man involved with the young movement for American freedom.

John and Samuel Adams, John Hancock, Paul Revere, and James Otis all come to life as we view them through the eyes of Johnny Tremain. The Boston Tea Party and the Battle of Lexington become a living drama as we better understand the humanity and history of the events leading to America's Revolutionary War.

1. How does the phrase "pride goeth before a fall" apply to Johnny and his burned hand?
2. Explain how reading a book like *Johnny Tremain* made you more aware of American history.
3. Compare the personality of Miss Lavinia Lyte to that of Cilla Lapham.
4. When Johnny realized that war would mean death to men on both sides, how did it affect him?
5. *Johnny Tremain* is called historical fiction. Which did you feel was its strongest point, its historical approach or its literary content?
6. Which of your projects did your group enjoy most?
7. How did your group demonstrate teamwork while completing the projects?
8. The late Esther Forbes bequeathed the royalties from the sale of her books to the American Antiquarian Society in Worcester, Massachusetts. Why do you think she did this?
9. Rate *Johnny Tremain* from 1 to 10 with 10 being the best.
10. Explain the term *a man can stand up* as it applies to this book.